THE TAO OF THE DUDE

Written, Edited and Illustrated by

Oliver Benjamin

Founder of The Church of the Latter-Day Dude (dudeism.com)

ABIDE UNIVERSITY PRESS

www.aui.me

Essay text, illustrations and cover design copyright © Oliver Benjamin

All rights reserved under International and Pan-American Copyright Conventions, including the right to reproduce this book or portions thereof in any form, except for use by a reviewer in connection with a review.

ISBN: 9781511520614

Published by:
Abide University
www.aui.me/press
Email: aui@dudeism.com

IMPORTANT NOTE TO READERS: This book is an independent and unauthorized fan publication. No endorsement or sponsorship by or affiliation with Joel and Ethan Coen, Jeff Bridges, Gramercy Pictures, or any other copyright and trademark holders is claimed or suggested. All references in this book to copyrighted or trademarked characters and other elements of *The Big Lebowski* are for the purpose of commentary, criticism, analysis, and literary discussion only.

Please send any questions or suggestions to totd@dudeism.com
Homepage for this book: www.dudeism.com/taoofthedude

About the author:
Oliver Benjamin is the founder of Dudeism (The Church of the Latter-Day Dude). A former journalist and graphic artist, he now devotes his full part-time to spreading the word of the Dude. Other stuff he does is here: www.oliverbenjamin.net

About Dudeism:
Dudeism is a philosophy/religion/what-have-you which may be many things to many people. However, most of us consider it a modern version of ancient Chinese Taoism which uses the film *The Big Lebowski* as its primary liturgical vehicle.
    Dudeism is not only the world's slowest-growing religion, but it is also possibly its least serious. Moreover, Dudeism is not antagonistic towards other religions and openly welcomes devotees of other faiths. Dudeism is compatible with any worldview that promotes peace, peace-of-mind, and doing no harm to others. One doesn't even have to consider Dudeism a religion, but we think it's more fun that way. Your *abideage* may vary. You can learn more about it at www.dudeism.com.

Table of Contents

Preface 5
  By the Dudely Lama

Ups and Downs, Strikes and Gutters 9
  The Big Lebowski and Taoism

This Aggression Will Not Stand 21
  Conflict

Our Basic Freedoms 26
  Liberty and Lifestyle

Just Take It Easy, Man 34
  Leisure & Relaxation

Some Kind of An Eastern Thing 45
  Zen Dudeism

Go Find a Cash Machine 54
  Money and Materialism

Are You Employed, Sir? 61
  Work

Keep My Mind Limber 69
  Intellect and Uptight Thinking

A Lot of Ins and Outs 76
  Open-mindedness and Creativity

That's Just, Like, Uh, Your Opinion, Man 84
  Pluralism and Tolerance

Can't Be Worried About That Shit 91
  Peace of Mind

And Proud We Are of All of Them 99
  Ambition and Achievement

A Worthy Fuckin' Adversary 109
  War and Politics

The Fuckin' Eagles, Man 118
  The United States of America

What's a Hee-ro? 125
  Heroism

A Wiser Feller Than Myself Once Said 134
    Knowledge and Education

New Shit Has Come to Light 141
    Progress

What in God's Holy Name Are You Blathering About? 148
    Religion

Careful, Man, There's a Beverage Here 157
    Spirits

A Pretty Strict, Uh, Drug Uh, Regimen 165
    Drugs

Strongly Vaginal, and a Pair of Testicles 175
    The Sexes

This Affects All of Us, Dude 184
    Idealism and Morality

The Preferred Nomenclature 193
    Language and Conversation

What The Fuck Are You Talking About? 199
    The "F" word

There's Not a Literal Connection 204
    Art, Literature & Film

The Whole Durned Human Comedy 213
    Funny Stuff

The Royal We 224
    Friendship and Community

It Really Tied The Room Together 230
    The Dudeiverse

Further On Down The Trail 236
    Dudevolution

This Was a Valued, Uh, Uh 241
    The Kerouac Rug Mystery

Preface

By the Dudely Lama

This is a religious book. But it is not sacred.

If you disagree with the subjects addressed herein, that's just like, your opinion, man. And that's cool. That's cool. Many learned me n have disputed these ideas.

However, we think there are many people who will dig its style. We hope it will really tie their room together and help make sense of the whole durn human comedy.

Together with introductory essays and illustrations which tie each chapter topic together, this book is a broad collection of "Dudeisms"—quotes, maxims, passages, and inspirational musings that help provide a frame of reference for The Church of the Latter-Day Dude, a religion more commonly known as *Dudeism*[1].

Dudeism's central holy text is the 1998 movie *The Big Lebowski*. A religion based on a movie? Since that seems silly to some people, we've decided to write this book so that our religion can be taken more seriously. Our expectations are modest.

The Big Lebowski is a movie about a man (nicknamed "The Dude") seeking recompense for a damaged rug, one which in his estimation "really tied the room together." Only, he never gets it. But what we, the audience, receive by the end of the film is a huge spiritual kickback: total enlighten-upment.

Like Homer's *Odyssey*, and God's *The Bible*, the Coen Brothers' *The Big Lebowski* is one of those stories which not only entertain and make you laugh and cry, but which provide a framework for living in a world which all-too-often pulls the rug out from under us.

Not everyone commends the film so strongly. *The Big Lebowski* proved a critical and popular failure upon its release in 1998, and there are still many people who think it's a pointlessly circular shaggy-dude story, one you have to be on drugs to appreciate.

However, those inclined to watch the movie a few times frequently come to realize that it is far more subtle, deep and far-reaching than they initially supposed. Like a threadbare but enchanted oriental carpet, *The Big Lebowski* offers up its magic only after time, patience and a certain limberness of mind.

Today, inching up on twenty years after its release, *Lebowski* is high in the running for greatest cult film of all time. What The Church of the Latter-Day Dude is in the process of doing is merely elevate this "cult" to relatively respected religion, just as the Romans did with Christianity and Tom Cruise did with Scientology. The

---

[1] www.dudeism.com

objective of this book is to help show that the ideas and attitudes illuminated in the film are far bigger and older than the story itself: They are universal, historical and philosophically far-reaching.

In other words, we contend that Dudeism is not some new shit that came to light; it has existed since the dawn of civilization, and that *The Big Lebowski* is only its New Testament. Well, this is a testament to that Testament. 3000 years of dudey-ful tradition, from Lao Tzu to Lebowski.

So what in God's holy name are we blathering about? Like any great religious manifesto, *The Big Lebowski* can be many things to many people. What we believe ties all the elements together is a profound spiritual inquiry which reveals a timely (though timeless) moral code, the manner for its time and place. It helps us fit right in there. And that's Dudeism.

Down through the ages, across the sands of time Great Dudes in History have served as a corrective to the problems civilization brings with it. And, in a nutshell, the way they did this was to roll through the game of life like a well-rounded bowling ball on a liberally lubricated lane. Of course, there were times when these Great Dudes were compelled to actively speak up and jot down a Port Huron Statement or yell objections like "What the fuck are you talking about?" or "This aggression will not stand," or "I'm sorry, I wasn't listening." But most often they merely lounged silently on the fringes of our cultural carpet, waiting patiently for the tides to turn while they do their best to keep their minds limber, or to just "take 'er easy" as possible under the circumstances. Whereas most religions these days have promised otherworldly paths of "liberation," the Dudeist league has plenty of lanes open in the here-and-now. It's your roll, Dude. Chop chop.

The square community may not give a shit about it, but Dudeism will always abide and keep on perpetuating itself. We happen to know that there are little Dudeists on the way. And we take comfort in that. Life should not have to stop and start at anyone's convenience but our own.

Now let's get down to cases: Each chapter of this book covers an important aspect of Dudeism and is titled by an appropriate line in *The Big Lebowski*. A brief ramble leads us off, investigating just what the film teaches us about the particular subject, featuring some old shit that came to light—historical what-have-you. After filling you in on the details, we've got certain information, man: a rich and varied collection of quotes by various dudes (and even a few *un*-dudes) which not only help illuminate the Dude attitude towards the subject, but also prove that despite the depth of our casualness, you're not dealing with morons here. While some sources stretch as far back as Plato and Lao Tzu and the Buddha, others are as recent as Lil' Kim and Steven Wright and Bill Hicks. Down through the ages, across the ampersands of time.

A wiser feller than ourselves (Jimi Hendrix) once said "In order to change the world, you have to get your head together first." Like any good rug, Dudeism provides a cushioning fabric to ground the floor of their being, a pattern which ties all the strands together, a fundamental nexus upon which to dance, drowse, and meditate. We got the venue we wanted. So come on over and give us notes. The bar's over there. See what happens.

Well, that about wraps 'er up. We sincerely hope that *The Tao of the Dude* really ties your ruminations together, that it helps provide the necessary means for a, necessary means for a *higher* education.

Abidingly,

Rev. Oliver Benjamin
The Dudely Lama of The Church of the Latter-Day Dude (dudeism.com)

*Care to extend the tradition? Got some good Dudeisms to suggest? Please visit dudeism.com/taoofthedude to contribute to the cycle.

The White Russian Tasters

UPS AND DOWNS, STRIKES AND GUTTERS

The Big Lebowski and Taoism

When we say that Dudeism has existed since the dawn of civilization, we're not just saying that it's really really old. We're saying that Dudeism came into existence *because* of civilization. Dudeism came about as a cooling corrective to the burning problems of mass society. More or less in the same way that the easygoing Dude corrects the violent tendencies of his obsessive, aggressive best friend Walter.

Most people are familiar with the Chinese Yin/Yang symbol. It looks sort of like a black fish and a white fish chasing each other around and around in a circle. What this symbol represents is a simple, universally-recognized concept, one alluded to in *The Big Lebowski* several times:

"Ups and downs, strikes and gutters."
"Sometimes you eat the bar, and sometimes the bar, well, he eats you."
"The Dude Abides."

The symbol tells us this: Change is the only constant. And to deal with it properly, we have to learn to abide—to take 'er easy, that is, in the calm center of the swirling storm.

You might have noticed that the logo of Dudeism is an updated version of this symbol—only instead of two fish, it contains two bowling balls (a strike and a gutter, perhaps, or merely the rotation of the ball as it rolls). This helps remind us that Dudeism's oldest ancestor is probably Chinese Taoism, the religion with which the Yin/Yang is associated. Of course, China is the the oldest continually-existing civilization in the world, so it's no surprise that Dudeism gets its start there. As far as we can tell, the first truly Great Dude in History was the creator of Taoism, Lao Tzu.

When Lao Tzu created Taoism 2500 years ago, human civilization was just coming into its adulthood, and like any confused and angry adolescent, it was suffering through turmoil and transition. Life in China at that time was so aggressive that it makes our current conflicts seem comparatively pacific.

A legendary sage who—like nearly every other major religious figure—may or may not have existed, Lao Tzu (literally "Old Boy") lived during what is called this "warring states" period of Chinese history. This was an age when each of the myriad kingdoms were at bitter war with each other. Rapid technological progress had facilitated the possibility of empire-building, and in the race to rule the world (well, parts anyway) there could be only one winner. Consequently, violence was so commonplace in China back then that some 50% of adult men could expect to die face down in the muck, to say nothing of their special ladies and children of promise.

Rather than abiding another moment in this horrible blood-soaked state of affairs, the celebrated sage Lao Tzu threw up his hands, said "fuck it" to his cushy government job and headed out West to go set up a private residence in a more mellow milieu. Before taking his leave, however, he scribbled down a short tome known to us now as the *Tao Te Ching*. As it turned out, the last testament of this goateed, robed and sandal-shod dude proved no less than a guide to living for all of humanity. Millennia later it is still high in the running for greatest self-help book ever written.

What's more, until recently, nobody even knew how meaningful his book actually was—the recent discovery of a more faithful copy has led to a far more detailed understanding of what Lao Tzu was really trying to say. Turns out, rather than some quasi-mystical book of poetic ruminations (as some had interpreted it), the old boy had provided a very logical set of precepts on how to truly "make life significant."

Essential to this "art of living" was the notion that one had to operate in harmony with the Tao—the natural "way" of our world's living systems. By "going with the flow" (in the parlance of our times) one could harness the power of nature and bring quality, depth, and duration to life. However, unlike other authors of world religions, Lao Tzu never spelled out exactly what that "way" was. Instead, the *Tao Te Ching* provided a series of principles which the reader could employ to help them live naturally (*Te*), in accordance with the natural way (*Tao*).

In other words, the Tao Te Ching is sort of a do-it-yourself manual, for yourself.

So what are the principles espoused in the Tao Te Ching? We'll briefly look at a few of them here—and in English, too. So you can *Tao* with a smile on your face without feelin' like the old boy gypped you. Furthermore, as Taoist ideas are unfolded throughout *The Big Lebowski*, the more you watch the movie, the more they'll *warsh* over you. If you sympathize with the Dude, you're on your way towards digging Taoism.

The Dude's Story

For those fortunate souls who have yet to enjoy the greatest movie of all time (our opinion), this is briefly what happens:

Unemployed 40-something ex-hippie Jeffrey Lebowski arrives at his modest Venice beach bungalow one night, only to be assaulted by two thugs. They demand money owed to a porn producer by the name of Jackie Treehorn, claiming Lebowski's wife has defaulted on a sizeable loan.

It is a case of mistaken identity. It is another Jeffrey Lebowski, a millionaire, whose wife owes Treehorn the money. Frustrated and angry, one of the thugs ("Woo") considers it appropriate to pee on Lebowski's Oriental rug. Lebowski considers this a serious offense, as he feels this rug really "tied the room together."

This punitive piss, as it turns out, sets an unlikely chain of events in motion. Lebowski (who prefers to be called "the Dude") attempts to get the other Jeffrey Lebowski to reimburse him for the rug, who at first refuses, and then decides to hire the Dude to help recover his wife, Bunny, who seems to have been kidnapped by Treehorn's thugs.

Well, that's the short of it, anyway. The long of it is the subject and concern of this book, and of our Dudeist faith.

Does the Dude achieve the modest task which is his charge? It doesn't really matter. Much to the chagrin of screenwriting teachers and everyday movie reviewers, the plot doesn't seem terribly oriented towards achievement, quest or closure. Though its surface narrative concerns the Dude's late-in-life effort to achieve something conventional cinema might recognize as heroic, he fails catastrophically, nearly every step of the way.

Indeed, it's not just that the Dude seems to accomplish virtually nothing in the film, but that evidently he hasn't accomplished anything in his whole life. Thus he is not anti-heroic, but rather, aheroic. Yet the movie assures us that this is not a problem: there is so much more here than the clichéd heroic imperatives in which most modern stories are invested: At its core *The Big Lebowski* is a satire on heroism, a farcical send up of a particularly American view of action, activism and achievement.

Like Lao Tzu boldly "giving up" on his society, the Dude comes off as ironically valiant in his renunciation of heroism: Through failure after bumbling failure, we come to see him as a truly exemplar individual, the only genuinely admirable character in the film. That's because while everyone else in the story is desperately struggling to be somewhere else in their lives, our "hee-ro" finds it preferable to remain stuck in his so-called rut. There never was any fucking *Macguffin* (Alfred Hitchcock's abstract term for the goal of a movie protagonist). The Dude was already where he wanted to be to begin with.

Perhaps we could have suspected this at the beginning, after he was introduced with a definite article before his name. Certainly "the" is a title far more assured than even "His Royal Highness," although the Dude does exude a certain royal nobility. And he is very often high.

Yet if his entrance wasn't inspiring enough, his exit at the end of the film borders on apotheosis, leaving us with his final coda: "The Dude abides." It is probably the most memorable line in a film which positively bursts with memorable lines. After all the crap that has happened to him, the Dude still abides—there is no better word for it—for he remains exactly as he did in the beginning, an incorruptibly gilded goldbricker. We take comfort in that because it means that despite our circumstances, with the right attitude we too might learn to do the same—keep on rolling calmly and smoothly despite the balance of gutterballs or strikes, before making it to the finals and being tossed into the bosom of the Pacific. Everything else is just notes on the Cycle.

Is that some kind of an eastern thing? Well, not far from it, actually. A way out East, there was a manual, a manual I wanna tell you about…

Woo Wee

It was almost certainly a conscious decision on the part of the Coen Brothers to have *The Big Lebowski* employ an actor of Asian descent named "Woo" to set the story in motion. Despite subsequent protests of the main character's best friend Walter, "The Chinaman" is definitely the issue here.

As it happens, *Woo* (normally transliterated as *Wu*) is probably the most important concept in all of Taoism and the *Tao Te Ching*. *Wu* can generally be translated as "emptiness" and tends to imply the value and power of vacant space. As the *Tao Te Ching* puts it:

> Thirty spokes unite in the hub,
> but the worth of the wheel will depend
> on the void where the axle turns.
> What gives a clay cup value
> is the empty space its walls create.
> Usefulness is to be found in non-existence.[2]

After urinating on the Dude's rug and leaving Lebowski's apartment empty-handed, Woo snarls to his fellow thug, "Fuckin' time waste." Despite his name and ethnicity, Woo is clearly not a practicing Taoist.

He's not alone in his estimation of the Dude. Almost all of the other characters in the film (other than the Dude) routinely pursue material wealth, social status or idealistic causes to fill a void which they evidently find painful. By their reckoning, since the Dude's life is utterly devoid of the stuff they all compulsively seek (money, possessions, a job, a family, a nice car, status, nice clothes), his entire life must be a "fuckin' time waste."

It is noteworthy that both John Lennon and Bertrand Russell independently came up with the aphorism "Time you enjoy wasting, was not wasted."

Dude Way

In contrast to the others, the Dude is perfectly content to lead a leisurely, uncomplicated and in many ways, empty lifestyle. It seems he enjoys his life precisely

---

[2] *Tao Te Ching*, James Legge version

because it is relatively empty—he puts *wu* into action. Or rather, inaction. Blissfully free of worry, obligation, and responsibility, even his leisure time appears conspicuously barren of purpose: he lounges about in his bathrobe, taking bubble baths, listening to recorded whale sounds, meditating to audio tapes of a five-year old bowling tournament, and gingerly recycling a few *tai chi* moves with a White Russian in hand. The only thing he seems to "work" at is competitive bowling, which is arguably the world's least athletic sport. And while everyone else at the bowling alley takes the competition all-too-seriously, the Dude appears to be in it largely for the fun and friendship. It's telling that despite this being a "bowling movie" we never actually see him, the main character, bowl.

More than just an escape from tribulation, the Dude's emptiness actually proves to be a source of great power and wisdom. There's a Zen Buddhist proverb which says that in order to fill your cup, you must first empty it. Put more prosaically: if you're full of shit then there won't be any space left for the good stuff when it comes along. This is why the cultivation of mental emptiness has long been the highest goal of most Eastern spiritual traditions. For one thing, it is the primary precursor to intellectual and spiritual insight. This is what the Dude refers to as "keeping his mind limber." Just as Woo's power comes from emptying his bladder, the Dude's comes from emptying his mind.

Thus, what at first appears to be a weakness in the Dude's character turns out to be his greatest strength. His flexible, non-prejudicial and ultimately accommodating nature allows him to perceive circumstances more clearly, which ultimately helps him solve the central (though rather unimportant) mystery of the movie. The Tao Te Ching says:

> A man is born gentle and flexible.
> At his death he is hard and stiff.
> Green plants are tender and filled with sap.
> At their death they are withered and dry.
> So it is that the stiff and unbending is the disciple of death.
> The gentle and yielding is the disciple of life.[3]

Though in his late forties, the Dude's mental apparatus still seems exceptionally youthful. He takes nothing for granted, has no preconceived notions and is always open to learning new things. This is shown most evidently in his tendency to repeat bits of dialogue from other characters just as a child would, in entirely new contexts to hilariously creative effect.

The Dude's consciousness tends toward a state which the Taoists call *pu*, or the "uncarved block"—that is, lacking a permanently carved inscription on the material of his mind. This allows him to approach each situation free of presumption, perhaps

---

[3] *Tao Te Ching*, translated by Gia Fu Feng, with edits by Denis Bider

sometimes even a bit naively. Yet like the green plants mentioned in the passage above, he is also limber and literally full of life.

Woo Way
The most common usage of "*wu*" in Taoist philosophy is in the compound *wu wei*, which can be translated as "actionless action" or "doing without striving." *Wu wei* asserts that if people are well-attuned to their surroundings and act with a clear awareness of what is required in any given situation, then excess energy will not be wasted and more harmonious results will follow from their actions. *Wu wei*'s prescription is similar to that of the famous Nike advertisement: "Just Do It." Only, in the Taoist (and Dudeist) version you're not obligated to purchase anything, and sometimes what you should "just do" is precisely nothing at all. Of course, if Nike had chosen the motto "Just Don't Do It" or perhaps "Just Dude It" they wouldn't have sold many shoes.

After the movie's inciting incident, the Dude "just does" whatever the situation calls for—he sort of shuffles along from situation to situation, seemingly without any real will of his own. And although lots of unfortunate things happen to him, he perseveres, and in the end solves the film's mystery; as the narrator puts it: everything more or less turns out alright. The Dude takes everything as it comes, goes with the flow, and tries to make the best of each circumstance. His story is a perfect illustration of the mechanics of *wu wei*, or as some of us Dudeists like to call it, "Dude Way."

Fuckin' A
The Dude himself concedes at the end of the film that life is full of "strikes and gutters." Yet the period of his life catalogued in the film falls mostly into the latter category: He fails to receive any of the monies promised him by various parties throughout the film; he loses his rug, a good friend and his car; and he is beaten up, mistreated and disrespected time and time again. Yet despite all these troubles, each time he resolutely regains his tranquil *atta-dude*. Moreover, by the end of the movie he has actually "achieved" considerably more than anyone else around him. His failures emerge as remarkably superficial when played against the broad and sweeping tragedies of his acquaintances and adversaries.

Thus, what we learn in watching the Dude through all the film's comic reversals and red-herrings is one of the most important principles of Taoism: It is not the things we accumulate, nor the things which happen to us that determine the quality of our lives, but rather the attitude we employ in dealing with the world. This is, of course, a reversal of the common propaganda of modern civilization, in which the tangible aspects of our lives are expected to inform the character of our intangible feelings.

As the Buddha himself put it not long after Lao Tzu, "with our minds we make the world." Yet all too often, we instead allow the world to make our minds. Commercials, peer pressure, social expectations, political rhetoric and our own ego insecurities all gang up to reverse this essential ancient wisdom for their own "fucking fascist" ends.

In a world gone crazy, the Dude skillfully manages to skip around obstructions in his path, just as he does in his own courtyard in the very beginning of the film. Half-and-half is not only an element in his favorite beverage, but in his rich and accommodating worldview as well.

Instead of seeing the Dude as incomplete, those that dig the Taoist style should realize the value of respecting what is empty, and unfinished and yet fulfilled and complete. Dudeism trumps the false dichotomy of optimists and pessimists when we see the glass as continually emptied and filled again. Just as the Dude himself adhered to a regimen that kept his mind limber, so did his Taoist Dudefather, Lao Tzu:

I am different from most people.
I drink from the breasts of eternity.

What's your drink Dude?[4]

---

[4] The illustration that heads up this chapter, called *The White Russian Tasters* is a parody of a famous Taoist painting called *The Vinegar Tasters* which was drawn centuries ago to illustrate the attitudes of the three great religions of China: Confucianism, Buddhism and Taoism.

In *The Vinegar Tasters*, Confucius, Buddha and Lao Tzu are all sampling vinegar from a barrel and their response to the taste is widely divergent. Since Confucius believes that life is sour, requiring many rules to correct it, his facial expression is puckered at the sour flavor. The Buddha believes life is bitter and full of suffering, so he grimaces at the vinegar's bitterness. Taoism's founder Lao Tzu, on the other hand saw life as essentially sweet and harmonious, so he finds it delicious and grins happily.

In our version, *The White Russian Tasters*, Donnie is frail and unworldly and so he gags on the harsh vodka and bitter coffee flavor. Walter is cocky and macho and so finds the sweet liqueur and creamy milk too cloying. But like a yin/yang, the Dude is at once juvenile and adult, masculine and feminine, sophisticated and simple. Thus he appreciates the complexity and contradiction of the whole curious cocktail. Like Lao Tzu, he also laughs as he enjoys his elixir.

What can it be that has fascinated such a variety of people for so long? How is it possible to contrive a book [The Tao Te Ching] in which everyone finds what he needs?
—Holmes Welch, *Taoism: The Parting of the Way*

In East Asia generally, the notion of a Supreme Being, so essential to Western religions, is replaced by that of a Supreme State of Being, an impersonal perfection from which beings including man are separated only by delusion.
—John Blofeld, *Taoism*

To Taoism that which is absolutely still or absolutely perfect is absolutely dead, for without the possibility of growth and change there can be no Tao. In reality there is nothing in the universe which is completely perfect or completely still; it is only in the minds of men that such concepts exist.
—Alan Watts

The clouds above us join and separate,
The breeze in the courtyard leaves and returns.
Life is like that, so why not relax?
Who can stop us from celebrating?
—Lu Yu

If you find yourself in a confusing situation, simply laugh knowingly and walk away.
—Jim Ignatowski, *Taxi*

He who is in harmony with the Tao is like a newborn child.
Its bones are soft, its muscles are weak, but its grip is powerful.
It doesn't know about the union of male and female, yet its penis can stand erect,
    so intense is its vital power.
It can scream its head off all day, yet it never becomes hoarse,
    so complete is its harmony.
The Master's power is like this.
He lets all things come and go effortlessly, without desire.
He never expects results; thus he is never disappointed.
He is never disappointed; thus his spirit never grows old.
—Lao Tzu, *The Tao Te Ching,* translated by Gia-Fu Feng and Jane English

Everything flows; nothing remains.
—Heraclitus

In a world of role-playing personalities, those few people who don't project a mind-made image—and there are some even on TV, in the media, and the business world—but function from the deeper core of their Being, those who do not attempt to appear more than they are but are simply themselves, stand out as remarkable and are the only ones who truly make a difference in this world. They are the bringers of the new consciousness. Whatever they do becomes empowered because it is in alignment with the purpose of the whole. Their influence, however, goes far beyond what they do, far beyond their function. Their mere presence—simple, natural, unassuming—has a transformational effect on whoever they come into contact with.
—Eckhart Tolle, *A New Earth*

Alas, the door of fortune does not open inward so that one can force it by charging at it; it opens outward and so there is nothing one can do.
—Søren Kierkegaard

When I do good, I feel good. When I do bad, I feel bad. That's my religion.
—Abraham Lincoln

I have a simple philosophy. Fill what's empty. Empty what's full. Scratch where it itches.
—Alice Roosevelt Longworth

The Linux philosophy is "Laugh in the face of danger." Oops. Wrong One. "Do it yourself." Yes, that's it.
—Linus Torvalds

Boredom is the feeling that everything is a waste of time; serenity, that nothing is.
—Thomas Szasz

If you learn to bend, then you need not break.
—Kwai Chang Caine, *Kung Fu: The Legend Continues*

I like life. It's something to do.
—Ronnie Shakes

Real action is in silent moments.
—Ralph Waldo Emerson

Surfing's not a sport, it's a way of life, you know, a hobby. It's a way of looking at that wave and saying, "Hey bud, let's party!"
—Jeff Spicoli, *Fast Times at Ridgemont High* (1982). Screenplay by Cameron Crowe

You've got to have rain in order to have a rainbow.
—Elvis Presley

The monk abandons the values of the greater society, as does the criminal, yet, in breaking the rules, one becomes a saint and the other a sinner.
—Thomas Moore, *Meditations*

There is nothing to it. But to do it.
—Sgt. Floyd Pepper, *The Muppet Show*

Today was good. Today was fun. Tomorrow is another one.
—Theodor Geisel (Dr. Seuss), *One Fish Two Fish Red Fish Blue Fish*

A man is born gentle and weak
At his death he is hard and stiff.
Green plants are tender and filled with sap.
At their death they are withered and dry.
Therefore the stiff and unbending is the disciple of death
The gentle and yielding is the disciple of life.
—Lao Tzu, *The Tao Te Ching*, translated by Gia-fu Feng and Jane English

The man who has given up desire
And moves without wanting anything,
Who says neither mine nor I
Wins peace.
No one sees the beginning of things
But only the middle
The end is also unseen
There is no reason to lament
—*The Bhagavad Gita*

Always do whatever's next.
—George Carlin

Nihilism is of two faces: active and passive nihilism. The former is the sign of a heightened power of the spirit, the latter a decline and regression of the power of the spirit.
—Joseph Campbell, *Creative Mythology*

It is something to be able to paint a particular picture, or to carve a statue, and so to make a few objects beautiful; but it is far more glorious to carve and paint the very atmosphere and medium through which we look, which morally we can do. To affect the quality of the day is the highest of arts.
—Henry David Thoreau, *Walden*

It is undoubtedly more comfortable to dwell in a well-ordered and hygienically furnished house, but that does not answer the question as to who is the dweller in this house, and whether his soul enjoys a similar state of order and purity, that is, like that of the house serving for external life.
—C.G. Jung, *Introduction to The Spiritual Teaching of Ramana Maharishi*

Taoism is a way of liberation, which never comes by way of revolution, since it is notorious that most revolutions establish worse tyrannies than they destroy. To be free from convention is not to spurn it, nor to be deceived by it. It is to be able to use it as an instrument instead of being used by it.
—Alan Watts, *The Way of Zen*

Whereas Confucius counseled his people to labor untiringly for the welfare and dignity of man in society, Lao Tzu and Chuang Tzu on the other hand cautioned them against excessive interference. In their view, the urge to change what by nature is already good only increases the sum-total of human unhappiness. These two urges: on the one hand to do something, and on the other hand, not to do too much, are forever contending in our natures. The man who can maintain a just balance between them is on the road to social and intellectual maturity.
—Arthur Hummel, foreword to *The Tao Te Ching,* translated by John C. H. Wu

Do what you can, with what you have, where you are.
—Theodore Roosevelt

The full-grown man sets his heart upon the substance rather than the husk.
Upon the fruit rather than the flower.
Truly, he prefers what is within to what is without.
—Lao Tzu, *The Tao Te Ching*, translated by John C. H. Wu

Tao is hard to define. An empty vessel that can be drawn from without needing to be filled. Bottomless. A deep pool that never dries.
—Camille Paglia, *Sex, Art and American Culture*

Strong and powerful men will bury themselves in earth
While the frail and gentle weaklings float above on currents of air.
—Lao Tzu, *The Tao Te Ching*

The Rules

THIS AGGRESSION WILL NOT STAND

Conflict

The Big Lebowski may be many things to many people: a detective caper, a critique of heroism, a parody of traditional film genres, or just a hilarious stoner romp. Perhaps more than anything else, though, it is a great *buddy film*.

All buddy films do the same thing: pair two wildly opposite characters together and wait for the fireworks. Then again, all types of films do this to some degree. That's because good stories rely on a tension between opposite characters, be they friends, enemies, or a combination of the two. After all, similarity is boring: without tension neither drama nor comedy can exist. As the *Tao Te Ching* teaches: without dark there can be no light, without love there can be no hate, without old there can be no young. And of course, without the *undude*, there can be no *dude*.

Characters in buddy movies may yank each other along a number of different axes. Examples include: Felix Madison and Walter Unger in *The Odd Couple* (fastidious/flatulent); Reggie Hammond and Jack Cates in *48 Hours* (madcap/mad); J.J. McClure and Victor Prinzim in T*he Cannonball Run* (macho/mincing); and Martin Riggs and Roger Murtaugh in *Lethal Weapon* (young and reckless/too old for this shit).

In Taoism's yin-yang symbol, we apprehend not only that the universe is made up of opposites, and not only that those opposites can indeed get along, but that those opposites in fact need each other to exist. Moreover, they carry the seed of the other within them—represented by the white dot in the black half and the black dot in the white—and often learn from each other as a result.

In *The Big Lebowski,* the easygoing Dude and his lunatic, Vietnam-obsessed buddy Walter couldn't be more different from each other. Had they met back in the 'sixties it's doubtful they would have found much common ground, and it's a good bet they would have clobbered each other from opposite sides of the fence with placards of protest and patriotism.

Even decades later in the early 90s, the point at which the film takes place, they still seem to disagree about everything. The beginning of act one, in which they argue over what to do about the Dude's stolen rug, is a virtual opera of comic outrage and perfectly-timed misunderstanding. At the end of this extended establishing scene, it turns out that all their cursing and yelling was a total waste of energy, and the only party who benefits is the giggling, appreciative audience.

Yet, like an old married couple, their bickering disguises an unshakeable affection. Though the Dude cannot believe what an asshole Walter is, and Walter condescends to what he perceives to be Dude's indolent naiveté, after each argument is over they immediately lapse back into a cool groove of mutual acceptance, harboring not the slightest grudge.

Though so-called marriage experts like John Gray and (his former wife) Barbara de Angelis may counsel otherwise, a good tussle may not always be a negative thing. When the combatants mutually respect each other, and boundaries are taken into consideration, a clash of ideas not only makes innovation and solutions to problems possible, but also reinforces friendships and can even make for a raucous good time.

Antagonism will never be expunged from the sphere of human existence, but our attitudes towards it can, and therein lies one of the lessons of both Taoism and *The Big Lebowski*—aggression will not stand, unless we elect to prop it up.

He who fights with monsters should be careful lest he thereby becomes a monster.
—Friedrich Nietzsche

You will not be punished for your anger. You will be punished by your anger.
—The Buddha

Violence is interesting. This is a great obstacle to world peace and also to more thoughtful television programming.
—P.J. O'Rourke, *All the Trouble in The World*

Better the man that conquer a thousand thousand men is the one who conquer one, himself.
—The Buddha

Moderate your desire of victory over your adversary, and be pleased with the one over yourself.
—Benjamin Franklin

Evolution in other animals had already hit upon a behavioral strategy that moderated fights between unrelated members of the same species, for example when two males competed for the same female. The golden rule was: Defend yourself if attacked, but don't be the aggressor, and stop fighting as soon as the other relents. Games theorists with computers took thirty years to identify this strategy; evolution needed more time, but found it repeatedly, and long before humans appeared on the scene the golden rule made many conflicts within species less lethal than they might have been.
—Nigel Calder, *Timescale*

In Lao Tzu's opinion no one can achieve his aims by action. How then can he achieve his aims? The answer was *wu wei*. "To yield is to be preserved whole…because the wise man does not contend no one can contend against him"…*Wu wei* does not mean to avoid all action, but rather all hostile, aggressive action…It is to make another person feel inferior that is the essence of aggression.
—Holmes Welch, *Taoism: The Parting of the Way*

Rancor emanates from a sense of inferiority. It is the imaginary suppression of the person whom we cannot actually suppress by our own efforts.
—José Ortega y Gasset, *Meditations on Quixote*

It is imperative to act in a rhythm different from that of adversaries. If your rhythm is incongruous, you can wade right in without your own defenses being crossed. Such a state of mind should also be savored as an object of reflective study.
—Yagyu Munenori, *The Book of Family Traditions On the Art of War*

The habits of the primitive—devotees themselves of restraint, diplomacy and negotiation—deserve relearning. Unless we unlearn the habits we have taught ourselves, we shall not survive.
—John Keegan, *A History of Warfare*

In a heart that is one with nature, though the body contends, there is no violence, and in the heart that is not one with nature, though the body be at rest, there is always violence. Be, therefore, like the prow of a boat. It cleaves water, yet it leaves in its wake water unbroken.
—Master Po, *Kung Fu (1972)*, Season 1, Episode 8. Script by Halsted Welles

Man somehow feels he is infinite, or rather that he is capable of desiring in an unlimited fashion; he desires everything, we might say. But he realizes that he is incapable of achieving what he desires, and therefore he must prefigure an Other (who possesses to an optimum degree what he most desires), to whom he delegates the job of bridging the gap between what is desired and what can be done.
—Umberto Eco, *Travels in Hyperreality*

Always forgive your enemies—nothing annoys them so much.
—Oscar Wilde

If there were in the world today any large number of people who desired their own happiness more than they desired the unhappiness of others, we could have a paradise in a few years.
—Bertrand Russell

Why is propaganda so much more successful when it stirs up hatred than when it tries to stir up friendly feeling?
—Bertrand Russell

Without contraries, there is no progression.
—William Blake

When I played pro football, I never set out to hurt anybody deliberately...unless it was, you know, important, like a league game or something.
—Dick Butkus

Que Ridiculo!

OUR BASIC FREEDOMS

Liberty and Lifestyle

"Man is born free but everywhere he is in chains" said that great pacifist, proto-dude, and general layabout Jean Jacques Rousseau. Rousseau maintained that man was basically good and that it was only society that made him evil. We didn't need more controls, therefore, but less! Greater freedom, the idea went, would allow everyone to act in accordance with their nature, which would lead to greater happiness and harmony amongst people. We shouldn't venerate kings and emperors, Rousseau maintained, but rather the "noble savage" of old.

It was a nice idea, but later studies proved the French philosopher wrong: "Uncivilized" tribal groups generally practice far more violence per capita than their civilian counterparts—up to twenty times more by some measures. Still, though Rousseau's argument had problems (beyond pacifism), it was fucking interesting, man. The Dude's compeers in his hippie days were—on a personal level—enormous fans. It conjured up a vision that the hippies quickly tried to emulate: savage nobility.

Though society, to survive, does in fact need people who "give a shit about the fucking rules," the hippies thought that maybe it would be easier to give a shit about them if there were fewer (or better) rules about which to give a shit. In other words, while Rousseau's fantasy about the traditional "noble savage" may have been fictional, with the benefit of education, technology and modern hygiene, the hippies endeavored to make it a groovy and functional lifestyle choice.

The hippie movement came and went, but the ideal of the noble savage continues to pop up again and again in the popular imagination. We see it in everything from the "natural" lifestyles of the leftist New Age movement, to the Ayn Randian anarchism of the Libertarian Right wing, to the technotopians who predict that once we become "100 percent electronic" all human conflict will be dead in the water. They may all be looking at the future through Rousseau-colored glasses, but the dream of total freedom is still alive and well.

What might a modern-day noble savage, look like, then? Well, we Dudeists have a pretty good idea: a guy who shops for half-and-half in his bathrobe and slippers; who doesn't put much concern in status because he doesn't even own a ladder; who may not abide by a list of God-given directions, but who practices the golden rule so regularly that it's become a reflex; someone like a Good Samaritan Egalitarian Barbarian—he avoids hurting anyone and helps out if he can, not because he worries about his immortal soul, but because it's easier and more rewarding in the long run than being a fucking asshole. We're talking about the Dude here.

The Dude shows how well this undressed attitude works in his dealings with others: Are you a cranky old cripple with a porno star for a trophy wife? "That's cool man." Are you a cowboy in a bowling alley who might just be coming on to him? "I dig your style too, man." Are you a screaming purple-clad pervert with a stuffed crotch claiming alpha-male status? Here the Dude's comeback is supernaturally kicked-back: "That's just like, uh, your opinion, man."

It's only when somebody's own freedom impinges upon the freedom of others that the Dude raises his shaggy hackles and waves his peace around—most notably, when he finds that the old man who shares his name (The Big Lebowski) is embezzling money from the charity named after him and which he administers. Here the Dude finally loses his cool and pegs him a "human paraquat"— paraquat being a chemical used to defoliate marijuana plantations. The Dude's accusation is the gravest he can muster, as vast landscapes of personal (and conceptual!) freedom are destroyed by the dope-killing chemical and for no good reason. Marijuana is a substance regarded by most scientists as essentially harmless to humans.

As a modern day noble savage, the Dude has effectively and elegantly opted out of most of society's expectations. By middle age he has acquired little money, never gotten married, done nothing with his college education, and he might not even be a very good bowler for all we know. Of course, one of the reasons some folks take issue with the Dude's lifestyle is that few societies could survive were all its citizens as idle as Venice Beach bum Jeffrey Lebowski.

But this misses the point—the standard he sets is not one of laziness necessarily, but of liberty. Not everyone could (or should, perhaps) be as slothful as the Dude, but it's sure nice to know it's a feasible choice, and one in which you might actually be little worse for wear—outside of your wardrobe, living arrangements and mode of transport, that is.

Noble savagery might not be for everyone, but our society would be better off at least knowing it's an option. Takes the edge off a little, doesn't it?

Moreover, as much as we like to venerate freedom, most of us wouldn't have the skill or fortitude to deal with so much of it. The Dude helps to remind us, as Janis Joplin put it, that "Freedom's just another word for nothing left to lose." When the Stranger says "It's good knowing he's out there, taking 'er easy for all us sinners" he acknowledges that sainthood isn't for everyone, and that no society could function were it populated entirely with saints. Nor with shaggy unemployed amateur bowlers. Then again, it's not as if Christians expect everyone to don tunics and wander around preaching the Gospels, either. Just as Christ is an idealistic and transcendent example to his followers, so is the Dude to his.

Perhaps it's not a question of entirely removing the chains which Rousseau saw everywhere around us, but being allowed to loosen them from time to time, to the point where we no longer really notice they're there. Let *The Big Lebowski* (and this book) remind you to regularly cut yourself some slack. To paraphrase Janis: Freedom's just another word for nothing left to *loosen*.

Be who you are and say what you feel because those who mind don't matter and those who matter don't mind.
—Theodor Geisel (Dr. Seuss), *Oh the Places You'll Go!*

Nature's fascism is greater than that of any society.
—Camille Paglia, *Sexual Personae*

Dreaming permits each and every one of us to be quietly and safely insane every night of our lives.
—William Dement

We are always getting ready to live, but never living.
—Ralph Waldo Emerson

He who has overcome his fears will truly be free.
—Aristotle

Like the nudist who imagines himself emancipated, but who has only become unbuttoned, such a misinterpretation of Zen freedom has mistaken a return to the irresponsible spontaneity of the child for a genuinely mature form of spontaneousness. Child*likeness* is not to be equated with Child*ishness*. The spiritual goal is not a giant step backward into a personal or primordial infancy, but the regeneration of one's Original Nature.
—Conrad Hyers, *Zen and The Comic Spirit*

You measure a democracy by the freedom it gives its dissidents, not the freedom it gives its assimilated conformists.
—Abbie Hoffman

A chaotic system can react to outside events much more quickly, and with much less effort, than a nonchaotic one. Living creatures must behave chaotically in order to respond to a changing environment.
—Ian Stewart, *Nature's Numbers*

Now, as everyone knows, it has only been in the last two centuries that the majority of people in civilized countries have claimed the privilege of being individuals. Formerly they were slave, peasant, laborer, even artisan, but not person. It is clear that this revolution, a triumph for justice in many ways—slaves should be free, killing toil should end, the soul should have liberty—has also introduced new kinds of grief and misery, and so far, on the broadest scale, it has not been altogether a success…It is bewildering to see how much these new individuals suffer, with their new leisure and liberty.
—Saul Bellow, *Mr. Sammler's Planet*

I wouldn't recommend sex, drugs or insanity for everyone, but they've always worked for me.
—Hunter S. Thompson

You can only be young once. But you can always be immature.
—Dave Barry

Few people are capable of expressing with equanimity opinions which differ from the prejudices of their social environment. Most people are even incapable of forming such opinions.
—Albert Einstein

I have an idea that some men are born out of their due place. Accident has cast them amid certain surroundings, but they have always a nostalgia for a home they know not. They are strangers at their birthplace, and the leafy lanes they have known from childhood or the populous streets in which they have played, remain but a place of passage. They may spend their whole lives aliens among their kindred and remain aloof among the only scenes they have ever known. Perhaps it is this sense of strangeness that sends men far and wide in the search for something permanent, to which they may attach themselves. Perhaps some deep-rooted atavism urges the wanderer back to lands which his ancestors left in the dim beginnings of history. Sometimes a man hits upon a place to which he mysteriously feels that he belongs. Here is the home he sought, and he will settle amid scenes that he has never seen before, among men he has never known, as though they were familiar to him from his birth. Here at last he finds rest.
—W. Somerset Maugham, *The Moon and Sixpence*

One of the elders said: Either fly as far as you can from men, or else, laughing at the world and the men who are in it, make yourself a fool in many things.
—Thomas Merton, *Wisdom of the Desert*

There are only two kinds of freedom in the world; the freedom of the rich and powerful, and the freedom of the artist and the monk who renounces possessions.
—Anais Nin

The truth will indeed set you free, but only if you recognize that there is more than one kind of truth.
—Ken Wilber, *A Brief History of Everything*

The older you get, the more rules they are going to try and get you to follow. You just gotta keep on livin', man. L-I-V-I-N.
—David Wooderson, *Dazed and Confused (1993)*. Screenplay by Richard Linklater

Peer pressure is the most powerful force in the universe.
—Kurt Vonnegut, *Palm Sunday*

Majority rule is a precious, sacred thing worth dying for. But, like other precious, sacred things, such as the home and family, it's not only worth dying for; it can make you wish you were dead. Imagine if all of life were determined by majority rule. Every meal would be a pizza. Every pair of pants, even those in a Brooks Brothers suit, would be stone-washed denim. Celebrity diet and exercise books would be the only thing on the shelves at the library. And—since women are a majority of the population—we'd all be married to Mel Gibson.
—P.J. O'Rourke, *Parliament of Whores*

The Supreme Court says pornography is anything without artistic merit that causes sexual thoughts; that's their definition, essentially. No artistic merit, causes sexual thoughts. Hmm...sounds like every commercial on television, doesn't it?
—Bill Hicks

It is easy in the world to live after the world's opinions; it is easy in solitude to live after your own; but the great man is he who in the midst of the crowd keeps with perfect sweetness the independence of solitude.
—Ralph Waldo Emerson

I just hate to be in one corner. I hate to be put as only a guitar player, or either only as a songwriter, or only as a tap dancer. I like to move around.
—Jimi Hendrix

Selfishness is not living as one wishes to live, it is asking others to live as one wishes to live.
—Oscar Wilde

Tyranny is always better organized than freedom.
—Charles Péguy

Necessity is an evil thing. But there is no necessity to live beneath the yoke of necessity.
—Epicurus

What Jefferson was saying was, Hey! You know, we left this England place 'cause it was bogus; so if we don't get some cool rules ourselves—pronto—we'll just be bogus too! Get it?
—Jeff Spicoli, *Fast Times at Ridgemont High (1982)*. Screenplay by Cameron Crowe

Life itself is the proper binge.
—Julia Child

Many people acting independently are more intelligent than a few people acting as a group. It is the difference between Princeton University and the Princeton University football team. Anyone who has been involved with even the smallest and most informal committee knows individuals make better decisions. A date is a kind of committee. Choosing what movie to see can be a herculean task for even the brightest couple.
—P.J. O'Rourke, *All the Trouble in the World*

Do not fear to be eccentric in opinion, for every opinion now accepted was once eccentric.
—Bertrand Russell

My choice is what I chose to do
And if I'm causing no harm, it shouldn't bother you.
Your choice is who you chose to be
And if you're causing no harm, then you're alright with me.
If you don't like my fire, then don't come around
'Cause I'm gonna burn one down.
—Ben Harper, *"Burn One Down"*

Now if 6 turned out to be 9,
I don't mind, I don't mind,
Alright, if all the hippies cut off all their hair,
I don't care, I don't care.
Dig, 'cause I got my own world to live through
And I ain't gonna copy you.
—Jimi Hendrix, *"If 6 Was 9"*

Limber

JUST TAKE IT EASY, MAN

Leisure & Relaxation

History is a record of the accomplishments of humanity, and is therefore not only incomplete but deceptive. This is because it is not only in our work, but also in our leisure activities that we discover what we, as humans, are really all about. Moreover, at leisure we do what we truly want to do, rather than what we feel we should or must do. Therefore, our free time might be more important to anthropology than our so-called "achievements." Sadly, scholarship seems to disagree. Few degrees or research grants are offered to those who might elect to study Leisure Science.

A lack of advancement on retreats has made it hard for us to take 'er easy. Given a good stretch of free time to enjoy, too many of us drop the ball, unsure what to do with our liberty. Too often we park ourselves in front of the TV and waste our hard-fought freedom by staring at product sales pitches and twit-chat with celebrities.

This is a tragedy of the grandest proportions. After centuries of toil and struggle modern man should have the wherewithal and fortitude to spend his free hours quite literally living it up—engaging in the activities that our souls cry out for, that lift the spirit, elevate the mind and rouse the body. Our vaunted "progress" is surely a misnomer if we are not nearly as adept at our play as we are at our work.

Perhaps it's because we're not very well-trained in the Arts of Ease that we are so lousy at them. As the Spanish philosopher Jose Ortega y Gassett suggested, "In due time pleasure will find its Newton." We should hope that this Philosopher of Fun will develop a Science of Spare Time to put an Epicurean Ethos into practice. In the meantime, at least we have the Dude, and inspiration from dedicated Dudeists such as the ones quoted in this book.

As richly themed as *The Big Lebowski* is, the multifaceted jewel in its crown which reflects all of the different aspects of the film is most likely the sport and art of bowling. Bowling reflects many of the film's more obvious aspects—Americana, multiculturalism, competition, fellowship, and most importantly, leisure. Bowling levels all playing fields, isn't necessarily taken too seriously, and brings people of all ages and backgrounds together but allows them to remain alone if they wish. It is one of the last examples of good, kind-hearted, friendly fun available in a leisure landscape overrun with expense, electronics, cockiness and cliques. What a shame it is that bowling alleys are going rapidly out of business. The landmark Star Lanes in which much of *The Big Lebowski* was shot closed down only a few years after the film was completed. (Tellingly, one of its wooden lanes was saved for posterity, reincarnated as a bar top in a pricey L.A. club with a dress code.)

Bowling aside, there are infinite other ways to spend one's free time wisely. Of course, even work can be considered play if it's something you love to do. Take the Dude's landlord Marty, for instance: His labor of love (the dance quintet, his "cycle") clearly took up a great deal of his spare time to concoct. And whether or not it was a worthwhile way to spend his free time is not for us to decide. We admire him not for the performance itself, but for *taking the time*.

Of course, sometimes the most creative form of leisure is just doing nothing at all—giving the mind time to wander gently, to rest, and to recharge its batteries. Just as with the body, limbering up the mind makes it work better and more pleasurably. It is for just this reason that Eastern spiritual traditions routinely prescribe daily meditation.

One suspects that the Dude's equanimity in the face of disasters and disappointments stems from familiarity with this ancient spiritual technique—years of committed relaxation practice. And while "doing nothing" may have its detractors, any Buddhist monk will tell you, to skillfully do so is no easy feat. It takes years of hard work to become so resolutely relaxed. Indeed the most profound achievement one can aspire to might be to create empty space and just "abide" in it. *Nirvana*, the mystical goal of all Buddhist practice, literally translates as "a place of nothingness."

Buddhists are not Nihilists, however. Were a Buddhist to admit he "believes in nothing" it would only mean he *believes* in it; that is, he has great faith in the power of emptiness.

In fact all religions preach the value of the void to some degree—that's because when we're free from distraction we can get that peaceful easy feeling that some people associate with things spiritual, rather than all the frivolous what-have-you that fills up the majority of our weekdays. The emptier a room may be, the more easily it can be illuminated.

"Enlightenment" can imply two different things after all – to cast light upon the unknown, or to just get rid of whatever was blocking the light in the first place. In this way, new shit comes to light, and it becomes much easier to take 'er easy.

Bowling is among the cheapest American fun to be had, where anyone at any level of skill can play without any degree of physical fitness or any of the typical trappings of 'jock' sports. Bowling is probably one of the least judgmental activities ever invented. At least for amateurs, it's more about having fun than keeping score.
—J.M. Tyree & Ben Walters, *BFI Film Classics: The Big Lebowski*

The Internet is a waste of time, and that's exactly what's right about it.
—William Gibson

One of the great paradoxes of our time is this great availability of leisure that somehow fails to be translated into enjoyment. Compared to people living only a few generations ago, we have enormously greater opportunities to have a good time, yet there is no indication that we actually enjoy life more than our ancestors did. Opportunities alone, however, are not enough. We also need the skills to make use of them. And we need to know how to control consciousness—a skill that most people have not learned to cultivate. Surrounded by an astounding panoply of recreational gadgets and leisure choices, most of us go on being bored and vaguely frustrated.
—Mihaly Csikszentmihalyi, *Flow: The Psychology of Optimal Experience*

In human life the struggle for existence has been in large measure replaced by the struggle for enjoyment.
—T.H. Huxley

If you never did you should. These things are fun and fun is good.
—Theodor Geisel (Dr. Seuss), *One Fish Two Fish Red Fish Blue Fish*

Life goes by pretty fast. If you don't stop and look around once in a while, you could miss it.
—Ferris Bueller, *Ferris Bueller's Day Off (1986)*, screenplay by John Hughes

Guard well your spare moments. They are like uncut diamonds. Discard them and their value will never be known. Improve them and they will become the brightest gems in a useful life.
—Ralph Waldo Emerson

The happiest part of a man's life is what he passes lying awake in bed in the morning.
—Samuel Johnson

Poetry can never be a substitute for war and murder, whereas games can be. A complete and genuine substitute.
—Aldous Huxley, *Eyeless in Gaza*

Half our life is spent trying to find something to do with the time we have rushed through life trying to save.
—Will Rogers

Secularist leaders spread more light by catering to men's leisure than by appealing to their minds. The churches were not different.
—Owen Chadwick, *The Secularization of the European Mind in the 19th Century*

The pursuit of truth and beauty is a sphere of activity in which we are permitted to remain children all our lives.
—Albert Einstein

Hard work pays off in the end, but laziness pays off now.
—Al Lubel

Let us read and let us dance—two amusements that will never do any harm to the world.
—Voltaire

Cultivated leisure is the aim of man.
—Oscar Wilde

I haven't had sex in eight months. To be honest, I now prefer to go bowling.
—Lil' Kim

There's never enough time to do all the nothing you want.
—Bill Watterson, *Calvin and Hobbes*

I never lose sight of the fact that just being is fun.
—Katharine Hepburn

Bed is the poor man's opera.
—*Italian proverb*

I loafe and invite my soul,
I lean and loafe at my ease...
Observing a spear of summer grass.
—Walt Whitman, *"Song of Myself"*

The trouble with dawn is that it comes too early in the day.
—Susan Richman

If you're too busy to go fishin', you're too busy.
—Jed Clampett, *The Beverly Hillbillies*

I love to sleep. It's the best of both worlds. You get to be alive, and unconscious.
—Rita Rudner

Far from idleness being the root of all evil, it is rather the only true good.
—Søren Kierkegaard

The early bird gets the worm, but the second mouse gets the cheese.
—Steven Wright

They talk of the *dignity of work*. Bosh. True work is the *necessity* of humanity's earthly condition. The dignity is in the leisure. Besides, 99 hundredths of all the *work* done in the world is either foolish and unnecessary or harmful and wicked. What people needed was not work: they needed values. To recite poetry, to contemplate pictures, to write or to talk briskly or to meditate and chew one's own thoughts, quietly, on the maintop—work was good if it made these things possible, and bad if it blinded one to them, or made them impossible…
—Herman Melville

My passions are all asleep from my having slumbered till nearly eleven and weakened the animal fiber all over me to a delightful sensation about three degrees on this sight of faintness—if I had teeth of pearl and the breath of lilies I should call it languor—but as I am I must call it laziness. In this state of effeminacy the fibers of the brain are relaxed in common with the rest of the body, and to such a happy degree that pleasure has no show of enticement and pain no unbearable frown. Neither poetry, nor ambition, nor love have any alertness of countenance as they pass by me.
—John Keats

If people concentrated on the really important things in life, there'd be a shortage of fishing poles.
—Doug Larson

Happiness is thought to depend on leisure; for we work in order to be at leisure.
—Aristotle, *Nicomachean Ethics*, Book X, Chapter 7

A man hath no better thing under the sun, than to eat, and to drink, and to be merry.
—*The New Testament, Ecclesiastes 8:15*

Leisure is a form of that stillness that is the necessary preparation for accepting reality; only the person who is still can hear, and whoever is not still, cannot hear … Leisure is the disposition of receptive understanding, of contemplative beholding, and immersion—in the real.
—Josef Pieper, *Leisure: The Basis of Culture*

Best actor alive? Are you serious? I spend most of my time avoiding work.
—Jeff Bridges, *The Guardian,* September 27, 2008

The feeling of being hurried is not usually the result of living a full life and having no time. It is on the contrary born of a vague fear that we are wasting our life.
—Eric Hoffer

Toot once, strum once
give us a song
    to Great Virtue.
enjoy yourself, relax
stop setting snares.
get delicate
    and follow
where that leads you.
go find a place to flop
and flop there.
—Kuan Han Ch'ing, *"Idle Wandering"* from *Wine Of Endless Life: Taoist Drinking Songs from the Yuan Dynasty,* translated by Jerome P. Seaton

Leisure is not justified in making the functionary as 'trouble-free' in operation as possible, with minimum 'downtime,' but rather in keeping the functionary human…and this means that the human being does not disappear into the parceled-out world of his limited work-a-day function, but instead remains capable of taking in the world as a whole, and thereby to realize himself as a being who is oriented toward the whole of existence.
—Josef Pieper, *Leisure: The Basis of Culture*

[Bertrand] Russell wanted not to redistribute wealth but to redistribute leisure and, thereby, the ability of all to practice any and all of the arts and intellectual pursuits and to enjoy any and all of the games and entertainments the culture has to offer.
—Tom Lutz, *Doing Nothing*

Even sleeping men are doing the world's business and helping it along.
—Heraclitus

The question isn't "what are we going to do," the question is "what aren't we going to do?"
—Ferris Bueller, *Ferris Bueller's Day Off (1986)*. Screenplay by John Hughes

Time is that which man is always trying to kill, but which ends in killing him.
—Herbert Spencer

Leisure is the Mother of Philosophy.
—Thomas Hobbes

In America, we hurry—which is well; but when the day's work is done, we go on thinking of losses and gains, we plan for the morrow, we even carry our business cares to bed with us…we burn up our energies with these excitements, and either die early or drop into a lean and mean old age at a time of life which they call a man's prime in Europe…What a robust people, what a nation of thinkers we might be, if we would only lay ourselves on the shelf occasionally and renew our edges!
—Mark Twain, *The Innocents Abroad*

Millions long for immortality who do not know what to do with themselves on a rainy Sunday afternoon.
—Susan Ertz

"I Don't Know Whether to Kill Myself or Go Bowling"
—Title of a country song by Thom Sharp

Funk is fun. And it's also a state of mind…it's all the ramifications of that state of mind. Once you've done the best you can, funk it!
—George Clinton

The bowling alley is the poor man's country club.
—Sanford Hansell

We are most nearly ourselves when we achieve the seriousness of the child at play.
—Heraclitus

Time you enjoy wasting, was not wasted.
—Attributed to both John Lennon and Bertrand Russell

Once there was a man who was afraid of his shadow and who hated his footprints, and so he tried to get away from them by running. But the more he lifted his feet and put them down again, the more footprints he made. And no matter how fast he ran, his shadow never left him, and so, thinking that he was still going too slowly, he ran faster and faster without a stop until his strength gave out and he fell down dead. He didn't understand that by lolling in the shade he could have gotten rid of his shadow and by resting in quietude he could have put an end to his footprints.
—Chuang Tzu, *The Complete Works of Chuang Tzu*, translated by Burton Watson

One isn't lazy about what one loves.
—Aldous Huxley, *Eyeless in Gaza*

Adventure. Heh. Excitement. Heh. A Jedi craves not these things. You are reckless.
—Master Yoda, *The Empire Strikes Back* (1980). Screenplay by Leigh Brackett

Nothing is so aggravating than calmness.
—Oscar Wilde

The Idler has no rivals or enemies. The man of business forgets him; the man of enterprise despises him; and though such as tread the same track of life fall commonly into jealousy and discord, Idlers are always found to associate in peace; and he who is famed for doing nothing, is glad to meet another as idle as himself.
—Samuel Johnson, *The Idler*

Do not put off till tomorrow what can be put off till day-after-tomorrow just as well.
—Mark Twain

My spirit seeks different food from happiness; for I think I have a suspicion of what it is. I have suffered wretchedness, but not because of the absence of happiness, and without praying for happiness, I pray for peace—for motionlessness—for the feeling of myself, as of some plant, absorbing life without seeking it, and existing without individual sensation.
—Herman Melville

Sometimes I fall asleep at night with my clothes on. I'm going to have all my clothes made out of blankets.
—Mitch Hedberg

It takes a lot of time to be a genius, you have to sit around so much doing nothing, really doing nothing.
—Gertrude Stein

42 – Leisure and Relaxation

If you can spend a perfectly useless afternoon in a perfectly useless manner, you have learned how to live.
—Lin Yutang

The Loungers are a remnant of the Epicurean sect; their pleasure comes from an absence of pain, and their business in having nothing to do. The life of a Lounger may perhaps with more propriety be likened to a dream, than that of other mortals.
—Abel Slug, *The Lounger's Miscellany*

I haven't slept for ten days, because that would be too long.
—Mitch Hedberg

Most people are in such a rush to enjoy themselves that they hurry right past it.
—Søren Kierkegaard

Early to rise and early to bed makes a man healthy, wealthy and dead.
—James Thurber

Idleness is the ideal of genius, and indolence the virtue of the romantic.
—Jostein Gaarder, *Sophie's World*

Many men go fishing all of their lives without knowing that it is not fish they are after.
—Henry David Thoreau

If Sloth Had Been the Original Sin We'd Still Be in Paradise.
—The J. Walter Thompson Advertising Agency, from a *Harper's Magazine* parody campaign promoting The Seven Deadly Sins

No ancient society before the Jews had a day of rest. The God who made the universe and rested bids us do the same, calling us to a weekly restoration of prayer, study, and recreation (or re-creation).
—Thomas Cahill, *The Gifts of the Jews*

Thus, any face which is fresh and graceful and reposeful, any really young face, is in Paris the most extraordinary of exceptions; it is met with rarely. Should you see one there, be sure it belongs…to the soft and happy race of loungers, the only folk really happy in Paris, which unfolds for them hour by hour its moving poetry.
—Honoré de Balzac, *The Girl With the Golden Eyes*

Cloud patterns are among the most powerful evokers of strong emotions, both positive and negative.
—Jerome Barkow, Leda Cosmides, and John Tooby, *The Adapted Mind*

An inert body can do no harm to anyone, provokes no hostility, is scarcely worth derision.
—Joseph Conrad, *Victory*

"Isn't it remarkable, Morten, how you can't get bored at the beach? Try lying on your back for three or four hours anywhere else—not doing anything, not thinking about anything."
—Thomas Mann, *Buddenbrooks*

A happy life must be to a great extent a quiet life, for it is only in an atmosphere of quiet that true joy dare live.
—Bertrand Russell

I never joined the army because at ease was never that easy to me. Seemed rather uptight still. I don't relax by parting my legs slightly and putting my hands behind my back. That does not equal ease. At ease was not being in the military. I am at ease, bro, because I am not in the military.
—Mitch Hedberg

The joy of living, I say, was summed up for me in the remembered sensation of that first burning and aromatic swallow, that mixture of milk and coffee and bread by which men hold communion with tranquil pastures, exotic plantations, and golden harvests, communion with the earth.
—Antoine de Saint Exupéry, *Wind, Sand and Stars*

I have sometimes amused myself with picturing a nation of loafers…Only think of it! an entire loafer kingdom! Adam was a loafer, and so were all the philosophers.
—Walt Whitman

To do nothing is the most difficult thing in the world. The most difficult, and the most intellectual.
—Oscar Wilde

Bearded, stern Jehovah gave his followers the supreme example of ideal laziness—after six days' work, he rested for eternity.
—Paul Lafargue, *The Right to be Lazy*

Dude Jitsu

SOME KIND OF AN EASTERN THING

Zen Dudeism

When you're trying to discuss something deep, it's often better to be indirect, vague, or even poetic about it. The problem with spelling things out is that people tend to get hung up on the words themselves and end up taking everything literally too literally as a result.

Like many of us, the Dude's pal Walter Sobchak is often infuriated by the struggles and sorrows in life, yet when he insists on connecting every single bummer to the Vietnam War, he loses his credibility and much of our sympathy. When the Dude calls his bluff, Walter grudgingly admits that "there's not a literal connection." But when Dude then insists that there's no connection at all, perhaps he's only half right. There is surely a symbolic link: Most of us fight little Vietnams every day of our lives. Stick-in-the-muck Sobchak just desperately needs a new metaphor.

Instead of speaking literally, sages throughout history have chosen to couch their teachings in poetry. That's because poetry makes the recipient an active participant in the quest for meaning, rather than just a passive consumer of prefabricated propaganda.

Of course, that often goes wrong as well. For instance, though most religious scholars regard the Bible as a collection of allegories, the majority of its fans take it at face value and follow it to the literal letter. It's a highly contradictory approach—though the biblical Jesus was outspoken against taking the Old Testament literally, his followers see no irony in doing the same with the New Testament, along with cherry-picked elements from the Old as well.

Of course, it's not just the western religions that lose their ability to actively interpret their own poetry. Buddhism was born in India in response to the strict and petty injunctions of Hinduism, but then went on to become heavily doctrinaire itself as new rules started to elbow their way in.

In an attempt to help Buddhism hew more closely to its more philosophical and spiritual origins, a sect was created in India called Dhyāna (Sanskrit for "meditation"). It rejected any written books or rules, preferring that its adherents employ direct experience and meditative techniques to plumb the deeper truths of existence. As The Big LeBuddhski spread itself across Asia, this little ragtag sect of anti-reactionaries followed in its wake, becoming *Ch'an* in China and finally *Zen* in Japan—the name by which we commonly refer to it in the West.

Though Zen isn't totally free of doctrine and dogma, it is high in the running for most philosophical and easygoing religion worldwide, probably coming in second only to Ancient Chinese Taoism (and by extension, of course, Dudeism). In fact some historians believe that Zen was actually an equal mix of Buddhism and Taoism. Traditionally, in fact, most of what Westerners (Alan Watts, for example) sympathize with in eastern philosophy comes from Zen and Taoism (and their Hindu counterpart, Yogism), not the preachy moral inunctions, socio-political engineering, and cumbersome polytheistic/animistic panoplies that actually make up the bulk of Eastern religion.

One is obliged to admit that a religion which puts sitting still and watching your mind wander at the center of its religious practice deserves to be regarded as pretty goddamn groovy. Aside from this practice, called *zazen*, Zen also employs some highly commended intellectual techniques to "open" the mind, the most famous of which is probably the *koan*.

A koan is a short, puzzling, often paradoxical idea which one is meant to contemplate as a way toward making sense of our contradictory, unfathomable world. It might be said that a koan is both a miniature poem and a puzzle.

One of the most famous koans is "If a tree falls in the woods, is there a sound?" Modern folks prone to materialist leanings might immediately answer yes, yet if we define "sound" as something that is perceived by a human being, then it's not so clear. Furthermore, if we define "sounds" as a vibration in space, then everything in the universe must be considered sound, including solid matter, and so the question becomes totally meaningless. So you see: there are a lot of ins and outs, a lot of strands in ol' Buddha's head. Thus, a strict koan regimen will help keep your mind limber, or at the very least provide good conversation while getting stoned with friends.

Yet koans don't have to be spoken by wise old Asian sages in order to be deep. In fact, they're all around us. One of the reasons people love to quote lines from *The Big Lebowski* is because they often resemble koans. Some kind of eastern thing? Far from it. There is accidental insight to behold everywhere if our eyes and hearts are open to it. The underbelly of the universe may appear to us everywhere: The world is full of contradictions, ironies, paradoxes, fingers pointing to answers that seem all but unreachable, yet which much be investigated if life is to surrender any meaning at all.

A famous Zen saying says "All instruction is but a finger pointing at the moon. To concentrate on the finger is never to see beyond." *The Big Lebowski* is chock full of those fingers—ideas and elements that inspire the viewer for no immediately obvious reason, yet lead us further down the trail of what it means to be human in a world where things are rarely what they seem to be.

In fact, the quotations in this very book should be considered a supplemental collection of such fingers—or perhaps more fittingly, toes.

More Lebowskian Koans:

- What is the sound of one hand jerking off manually?
- Does a Pomeranian have a Buddha nature?
- Show me the business papers of an unemployed man.
- Like this cup, you are full of just like, your opinions, man. There are ways, Dude. But stay, enjoy your coffee. This is a family restaurant.
- Show me your original handle, the one you had before the one your ever-lovin' parents gave you.
- What makes a man, Li Bao Xi?
- No-mind if I un-burn a jay?

Into the skies one summer's day,
I sent a little thought away,
Up to where in the blue round
The sun sat shining without sound.
   Then my thought came back to me—
Little thought, what did you see?
In the regions whence you came?
And when I spoke, my thought was dumb.
   But she breathed of what was there,
In the pure bright upper air.
And because my thought so shone,
I knew she had been shone upon.
—William Brighty Rands, *"The Thought"*

I am against nature. I don't dig nature at all. I think nature is very unnatural. I think the truly natural things are dreams, which nature can't touch with decay.
—Bob Dylan

He who wonders discovers that this in itself is wonder.
—M.C. Escher

Now is the time for all good men to come to.
—Walt Kelly

And remember, no matter where you go, there you are.
—Buckaroo Banzai, *The Adventures of Buckaroo Banzai Across the 8th Dimension (1984)*. Screenplay by Earl Mac Rauch

My son has taken up meditation. At least it's better than sitting doing nothing.
—Max Kauffman

I didn't come here and I ain't leavin'.
—Willie Nelson

He was back to zero again, and now those things were gone. For even the smallest zero had a great hole of nothingness, a circle large enough to contain the world.
—Paul Auster, *The Music of Chance*

Time isn't measured by length but by depth.
—Isolde Kurz

The nature of reality is a process, a continuously changing flow. Nothing is absolute; it is always changing. The realization of this process is what the Zen practitioner is trying to attain. Experiencing this flow, this process directly, personally and immediately is what is meant by "being within the moment."
—Musashi, *The Book of Five Rings*

If you want to be happy, be.
—Leo Tolstoy

There is nothing so stable as change.
—Bob Dylan

It's great to be here. It's great to be anywhere.
—Keith Richards

A person starts to live when he can live outside himself.
—Albert Einstein

How long has it been since I came up here to live?
When tired, I stretch my legs for a nap
Inspired, I put on my sandals and go for a walk
People in the world can think what they like
Laughter or praise, it's all the same
My mother and father gave me this life
I'm naturally happy, whatever comes my way.
—Ryokan

Coincidences are spiritual puns.
—G.K. Chesterton

Carlos Castaneda once told me bathrooms are dangerous places. If one gets "silent" enough on the bowl, a crack in the world opens up.
—Bruce Wagner

Do each act as though it were your last, freed from every random aim, from willful turning away from the directing Reason, from pretense, self-love and displeasure with what is allotted to you.
—Marcus Aurelius

Tom Seaver: Hey Yogi, what time is it?
Yogi Berra: You mean now?

Q: How many Zen Masters does it take to change a lightbulb?
A: None. The lightbulb is always changing. The Zen Master just sits there.
—Unknown

#3530. That which does not appear to exist is to be regarded as if it did not exist.
—California Civil Code, "Maxims of Jurisprudence"

For me, the lame part of the Sixties was the political part, the social part. The real part was the spiritual part.
—Jerry Garcia

The reverse side also has a reverse side.
—Japanese proverb

Life is not a problem to be solved, nor a question to be answered. Life is a mystery to be experienced.
—Alan Watts

A moment's insight is sometimes worth a life's experience.
—Oliver Wendell Holmes

A commonly recognized trait of fools is that they are a distinguished form of sage.
—Conrad Hyers, *Zen and the Comic Spirit*

There ain't no answer. There isn't going to be any answer. There never has been an answer. That's the answer.
—Gertrude Stein

Nothing is real to us but our hunger, nothing sacred but our own desires.
—Okakura Kakuzo, *The Book of Tea*

One of the many lessons that one learns in prison is, that things are what they are and will be what they will be.
—Oscar Wilde

What if everything is an illusion and nothing exists? In that case, I definitely overpaid for my carpet.
—Woody Allen

We are what we think
All that we are arises with our thoughts
With our thoughts we make the world.
    Speak or act with an impure mind
And trouble will follow you
As the wheel follows the ox that draws the cart
    Speak or act with a pure mind
And happiness will follow you
As your shadow, unshakable
—The Buddha, *The Dhammapada*, rendered by Thomas Byrom, 1976

And so the typical structure of experience is like a punch in the face. The ordinary self is the battered self—it is utterly battered by the universe "out there." The ordinary self is a series of bruises, of scars, the results of these two hands of experience smashing together. This bruising is called "duhkha," suffering. As Krishnamurti used to say, in that gap between the subject and the object lies the entire misery of humankind.
—Ken Wilber, *A Brief History of Everything*

The Zen people call it the "sound of one hand clapping." Now, one hand clapping cannot create a sound; it is a soundless sound, the *omkar*, just silence. But silence is not empty, it is very full. The moment you are absolutely silent, absolutely attuned with nothingness, the whole descends in you, the beyond penetrates you.
—Osho, *Death, The Greatest Fiction*

Under the tree the shade is pleasant; out in the open the heat is scorching. A person who has been going about in the sun feels cool when he reaches the shade. Someone who keeps on going from the shade into the sun and then back into the shade is a fool. A wise man stays permanently in the shade. Similarly the mind of one who knows the truth does not leave *Brahman*.
—Ramana Maharishi, *The Spiritual Teaching of Ramana Maharishi*

Another analogy might be that dreams, like the stars, are shining all the time. Though the stars are not often seen by day, since the sun shines too brightly, if, during the day, there is an eclipse of the sun, or if a viewer chooses to be watchful awhile after sunset or awhile before sunrise, or if he is awakened from time to time on a clear night to look at the sky, then the stars, like dreams, though often forgotten, may always be seen.
—Carl Sagan, *The Demon-Haunted World*

I love you when I forget about me.
—Joni Mitchell

Paradise, for Zen, is immediately accessible and is indistinguishable from the world of ordinary perception—though not as ordinarily perceived. It is not to be located in some other world, nor in a world which one enters by closing the eyes and shutting out the mundane and the commonplace, nor a world which by its holiness and infinity and brilliance devalues this world, empties it, and renders it impure, drab and profane. It is not the world at the end of the rainbow of fantasy and mind-expansion, or at the furthest remove from this world…As Dogen, the founder of Japanese Soto insisted, one should "just sit" for there is nowhere to go and nothing to achieve. There is no mountain to conquer, no spiritual ladder to climb, no river to cross.
Conrad Hyers, *Zen and The Comic Spirit*

Some who live are dead and some who are dead are alive.
—Bob Marley

Each man must look to himself to teach him the meaning of life. It is not something to be discovered: it is something moulded.
—Antoine de Saint Exupéry, *Wind, Sand and Stars*

Our dominating fears and desires have become so familiar to us that we do not even notice them; they are like recurring drumbeats going on in the background of our thoughts. And so, as a preliminary exercise, it is good to spend some time every day simply watching our minds, listening to those drumbeats. We probably shall not like what we see and hear, but we must be very patient and objective. The mind, finding it watched in this way, will gradually grow calmer. It becomes embarrassed, as it were, by its own greed and silliness. For no amount of outside criticism is so effective and so penetrating as our own simple self-inspection.
—Christopher Isherwood, *How to Know God: Patanjali's Yoga Sutras*

The Good with the Bad

GO FIND A CASH MACHINE

Money and Materialism

"Money makes the world go 'round!" has become one of our most beloved modern day sayings, having neatly supplanted the former world-turner, "love." These days, without enough money to properly "feed the monkey," love weakens and often strays. Sometimes it even gets involved with known pornographers.

With money on the forefront of people's minds these days, it's hard to believe that for the vast majority of the whole durn human comedy, money didn't even exist. What in God's holy name did people blather about back then?

Most likely, folks sat around telling stories about monsters or how people in other tribes weren't actually human or about how the gods cheated on each other. In other words, serious fears and concerns, laughable as they might seem today.

Yet in today's literature, nearly every novel or movie has cold hard cash as its primary goal; if not getting more money, then holding on to love or self-respect despite the lack of money. Money is no longer the root of all evil – it's the root of all everything.

The Big Lebowski is no exception, though its take on the nature of money is breathtakingly fresh—in its uniquely ironic and Zen-like fashion, the actual money pursued in the movie turns out to be an illusion. Here's the entire story of *The Big Lebowski* broken down into a Zen conversation:

> *Student: Where's the money, Lu Bao Xi?*
> *Master: There never was any fucking money.*
> *Student: That's fucking interesting.*
> *Master: You're not dealing with Mongols here.*

Of course, anyone who has witnessed the economic tumult of the early 21st century has some inkling that this is in fact the case. Money is more illusory than many of us had even realized. Here's a koan:

If money disappears in the Bretton Woods, does it exist?

Bretton Woods, of course, was the conference in which world leaders decided that in order to anchor the value of money in reality, symbolic cash had to be tied to something physical—namely gold reserves. That is, until Nixon (the Dude's former adversary) decided that money was in fact an idea, and not a thing. After which, being a nation of impossible dreamers, America became very rich. Of course, as any religious leader should be aware, ideas are far more powerful than actual things, unwieldy as they may be to operate.

It should come as no surprise, therefore, that it was at this point—when money became abstracted into an idea—that we can say that finance replaced religion as the dominant faith in the developed world. Instead of believing that an invisible God on a cloud was commanding us, it was now Adam Smith's "invisible hand" of market dynamics that was doing all the blathering. Got a problem with that? Talk to the invisible hand.

It should therefore come as no surprise that humans have an ambivalent love-fear relationship with money, given that it commands the power God once wielded. On one hand, it is the greatest labor-saving device in history, affording us freedoms and conveniences unimaginable to our distant ancestors. On the other hand, like Pandora's Box it also unleashes all sorts of troubles upon our conscience and our relationships with other people.

Aside from everything else that *The Big Lebowski* may be classified as, the film is also an astute study of the Pandora-like problems which money introduces into human life. With the Dude acting as the only agnostic, we are made privy to the myriad ways in which Moneytheism buys and sells the soul: The wholesome Midwestern cheerleader now offers blowjobs for $1000; the musician/nihilist abandons philosophy and creativity to become a porn star/scam artist; the ambitious businessman adopts banditry in order to camouflage his own incompetence; the liberated artist/feminist morphs into a haughty and self-serving succubus; the crusading soldier degenerates into a petty mercenary. And on and on.

So it's not just Walter who throws out ringers of dirty undies in the hopes of exchanging them for easy cash. Everyone in the movie is guilty of this empty pretense, except for the Dude, of course. He is "not trying to scam anyone," and genuinely only wants to get back what was rightfully his in the first place: his rug. Given that money is power, and that he has none, he is in a unique position to fail in this quest.

Yet despite the inequities evinced in the film, economics is not the issue here. Dudeism is not especially concerned with the distribution of wealth or the rules of its acquisition. Rather, what should concern us is only peace of mind. Though money is meant to act as a palliative, it often has the unexpectedly opposite effect. The only person in the film who appears happy is the one who has the least to his name. Yet according to science, this should come as no surprise: Psychologists have shown time and again that as long as life's necessities are covered, people don't need a surplus of money to be happy. There is virtually no evidence that "rich fucks" are on average any more cheerful or content with the quality of their lives than "deadbeats," "goldbrickers" or any others without the necessary means for a necessary means.

What's worse, studies have proven that financial-based happiness is the most pernicious of illusions: people are only financially content when they think they have at least as much as their friends and neighbors do. Peer pressure, as Kurt Vonnegut has pointed out, is the strongest force in the universe. And like other universal forces, it is deaf, dumb, and blind to human contentment. It sure plays a mean pinball. But perhaps we can elect to opt out of the game. Parts, anyway.

Most people admit that they'd love to have more free time to spend with their children, to play, and to just do nothing. They could do this rather easily if they made some important sacrifices: Stop buying so much stuff, eating so much crap and throwing so much away. Of course it sounds pat, but the slew of "simplify your life" guides on bookstore shelves these days prove that it's not only pressing, but possible.

Many viewers of *The Big Lebowski* are baffled by the Dude's ability to work so little and live fairly comfortably, objecting that the character's lifestyle is unrealistic. Yet while bungalows in Venice, CA today are accessible only to highly commended artists and known pornographers, back in 1991 rents were low enough that a part time laborer or temporarily unemployed beach bum could make do so long as he or she lived simply. Aside from the requisite bottle of Kahlua liqueur and a modest quota of marijuana, the Dude admits few premium indulgences.

Most religions feature a story where its hero (Buddhism and Christianity furnish the best examples) is tempted to abandon the righteous path. Dudeism is no different. When the Dude's own naïve, trusting nature leads him to open up a Pandora's Box of his own, his comfortably laid-back life begins to fray at its well-worn seams. Promised some easy dough in exchange for a shady job, it is not long before the Dude is in over his head and all the trouble in the world lands in his lap. But after sacrificing his principles in a quest for cash and closure, he finally manages to snap back and free himself from this "uptight thinking" in order to solve the caper.

It is a resurrection of sorts, although his trajectory is back down to earth rather than heavenward. At story's end, the Dude returns to his old life with nothing to show for it other than the knowledge that his frugality may well be the greatest asset he owns. As Epicurus maintained, "A man is wealthy in proportion to the things he can do without."

In the end, the Dude reaffirms what he knew already: rather than make the world go 'round, money just makes the whole world go fucking crazy.

We all pay for life with death, so everything in between should be free.
—Bill Hicks

My head is not in the material world. I am a man who sleeps on stone. Go into the hills and rest. That's my pleasure. I own the earth, you know, all things belong to I.
—Bob Marley

What right-thinking individual would spend hours, *hours* every evening watching advertisements? Is it not clear that a product which must spend fortunes drawing attention to itself is probably not one we need?
—David Mamet, *Three Uses of the Knife*

America's greatest troubles come from the advertising business…It makes people want to buy things that they would not otherwise want to buy. It fills their minds with desire for ingenious devices and with ambition to have more than their neighbors.
—Holmes Welch, *Taoism: The Parting of the Way*

A table, a chair, a bowl of fruit and a violin; what else does a man need to be happy?
—Albert Einstein

When he tries to extend his power over objects,
Those objects gain control over him.
He who is controlled by objects
Loses possession of his inner self.
—Chuang Tzu, *The Way of Chuang Tzu*, translated by Thomas Merton

To be satisfied with little is hard, to be satisfied with a lot impossible.
—Marie Von Ebner-Eisenbach

Frugality makes one independent.
—Theodora Lau, *Best Loved Chinese Proverbs*

Stuff is important. You gotta take care of your stuff. That's what life is all about: trying to find a place for your stuff. That's all your house is: a place to keep your stuff. If you didn't have so much stuff, you wouldn't need a house. You could just walk around all the time.
—George Carlin

How immaterial are all materials!
—Herman Melville, *Moby Dick*

The price we pay for money is paid in liberty.
—Robert Louis Stevenson

I have the world's largest seashell collection. You may have seen it, I keep it spread out on beaches all over the world.
—Steven Wright

If everyone demanded peace instead of another television set, then there'd be peace.
—John Lennon

Material standards are only the basis for fuller development, the necessary foundation on which further possibilities of knowledge and enjoyment may be realized: for to concentrate on material standards alone would inevitably degenerate into a scramble for material goods, unless it is transcended by the more inclusive motive of realizing total human possibilities.
—Julian Huxley, *New Bottles for New Wine*

You never know what is enough until you know what is more than enough.
—William Blake, *The Proverbs of Hell*

The danger is not mere exposure to occasional violent or prurient images but the acceptance of a degraded environment that devalues everything—a shadow world in which our kids are breathing in an awful lot of poison without knowing that there's clean air and sunshine elsewhere. They are shaped by the media as consumers before they've had a chance to develop their souls.
—David Denby, *"Buried Alive,"* New Yorker Magazine, July 15, 1996

Avarice is the sphincter of the heart.
—Matthew Green

What good is money if it can't inspire fear in your fellow man?
—Montgomery J. Burns, *The Simpsons* (Season 3, Episode 11. Script by John Vitti)

Money often costs too much.
—Ralph Waldo Emerson

Whoever possesses little is possessed by that much less.
—Friedrich Nietzsche

Riches do not exhilarate us so much with their possession as they torment us with their loss.
—Epicurus

I don't care about losing all the money. It's losing all the stuff.
—Marie Kimble Johnson, *The Jerk (1979)*. Screenplay by Steve Martin, Carl Gottleib and Manny Elias

You can tell the ideals of a nation by its advertisements.
—François-René de Chateaubriand

You can't have everything. Where would you put it?
—Stephen Wright

We can never have enough of that which we really do not want.
—Eric Hoffer, *The Ordeal of Change*

A man is rich in proportion to the number of things which he can afford to let alone.
—Henry David Thoreau

If money be not they servant, it will be thy master. The covetous man cannot so properly be said to possess wealth, as that may be said to possess him.
—Francis Bacon

It is said that for money you can have everything, but you cannot. You can buy food, but not appetite; medicine, but not health; knowledge but not wisdom; glitter, but not beauty; fun, but not joy; acquaintances, but not friends; servants, but not faithfulness; leisure, but not peace. You can have the husk of everything for money, but not the kernel.
—Arne Garborg

There ain't no such thing as a free lunch.
—Robert A. Heinlein, *The Moon Is a Harsh Mistress*

The money you have gives you freedom; the money you pursue enslaves you.
—Jean Jacques Rousseau

Obstacles Overcome

ARE YOU EMPLOYED, SIR?

Work

According to physics, to work is to break the basic laws of the universe. Thus the harder you work, the more criminal you shall be.

It's quite the cosmic joke: the second law of thermodynamics states that the universe must break down—complex molecules and all other systems are gradually falling apart. Theoretically, way off in the distant future, the universe should end up as an ethereally thin soup of celestial sameness. At that point there would be nothing to worry about because there will be no things.

Or, at least, it would be that way if a certain rogue element hadn't gotten together and accidentally invented work. The guilty party? Life itself. And since we work harder than any other living thing on earth, humans are the de facto kingpins of the organized crime syndicate.

In physics, the term "work" literally means to transfer energy from one system to another by force. In this sense, work as we know it began with the dawn of life on our planet: By transferring the energy of the sun and directing that energy inwards to build structures that reproduced themselves, living systems evolved complexity out of nothing. In doing so, they brazenly thumbed their nose at one of the oldest injunctions in the universe. To a sentimental physicist with a fondness for metaphor, this would have been the original fall from grace.

Buddhists say that "all life is suffering," and it's no wonder—life knows it's a scofflaw and, down deep, probably feels pretty bad about it. In fact, the Buddhist quest for stillness, non-attachment and ultimately *nirvana* (literally a place of vacation) in fact seems to be an attempt to vainly counteract our planet's bizarre and vaguely cancerous malediction, work.

It's no surprise that humans suffer more than any other creature. In making such a sacred institution of labor, we go one step further than other living things—our entire society is founded on flagrantly breaking the second law of thermodynamics, mostly just for the hell of it. The more gratuitously we break the law, the more we are likely to ultimately feel some sort of remorse. No one on their deathbed says "I really should have worked more in my life."

The famous Greek myth of Sisyphus concerns a man forced to roll a huge rock up a hill again and again for no good reason. The story is commonly used by writers to illuminate any of the pointless struggles that humans are saddled with. In his book *The Myth of Sisyphus,* philosopher Albert Camus suggested that our cultural imperative to continually "move forward" is pointlessly Sisyphean since we can never be satisfied, there is no end game, and ultimately it only brings us closer to death.

It wasn't always so bad: Humankind's relationship with work has gradually degraded over the eons. Twenty thousand years ago, our hunter-and-gatherer ancestors toiled very little—picking roots and vegetables and killing a few animals from time to time. After agriculture was discovered, we worked a bit harder, but only for parts of the year; the rest of the time we just watched the grass grow. After that, civilization took hold, and with it came wars and inequity, and more and more people were forced to work a lot for very little return. That's when our troubles really got started. It got so bad during the industrial revolution a couple hundred years ago that people dropped dead at thirty years old from overwork and poisoning from industrial toxins. Darkness literally warshed over.

But the smoke has since cleared quite a bit and with today's modern technologies doing much of the heavy lifting, it's now possible for people in the "developed" world to live longer lives with greater security than our ancestors, and do so with not much effort at all.

The crazy thing is that despite this, most of us lucky heirs to history now work harder than ever, wasting the best hours of our lives on activities we hate to do.

There are many possible reasons for this, among them: keeping up with peers, the lust for shiny new products, commercial propaganda, and an inadequate understanding of the nature of happiness. Although some of the reasons are hard-wired, like pecking order and territorial instincts, many are merely imposed on us by our cultures—several perfectly decent parts of the world have nothing at all resembling a work ethic.

Thus it is the duty of crusading dudes everywhere to struggle against *the crime of overtime*: which, by our estimate, means doing anything you don't want to do for more than four hours a day (ideally, less). The universe will reward you for it with peace of mind, lower blood pressure, pleasant memories and possibly even longer life. You won't be able to buy as much iCrap as other folks, but you'll have way more time to do things like go bowling and engage in natural, zesty enterprises.

In the beginning of *The Big Lebowski*, the wealthy old Lebowski admonishes the Dude: "My advice to you is do what your parents did—get a job, sir!" When the Dude puts on his sunglasses and retorts "ah, fuck it" the protest is not only his alone—an indignant universe is speaking through the Dude like Jehovah via the burning bush. Here is its straight dope: "Some things are more trouble than they're worth."

Had the Dude long ago heeded similar career advice and more assiduously pursued gainful employment, there might have been little to distinguish the two

Lebowskis. And fom the Dudeist point of view, this would have been a felony of cosmic proportions.

Environmentalists (and the bad guys in the movie *The Matrix*) have suggested that the human race is a sort of an infection of our ecosystem which destroys healthy natural patterns for selfish reasons. In other words, we're pissing on the foundation which ties the room (all of it) together.

Just as living creatures consume to survive, powerful economies consume to thrive. And since big cats and tiny bacteria are no longer so good at killing us off, our whole ecosystem is out of whack. Our world is poised to die from overwork and overconsumption. Hooray for environmental activists, of course, but let's not disregard the contributions of those lazy men and women who are "takin' er easy for all us sinners." They may just be the unsung heroes of the apocalypse.

Student: Why do the bums always lose?
Master: Because they don't play the game.
Student: That's fucking interesting.
Master: Shut the fuck up, Dong Ni.

Children are smarter than any of us. Know how I know that? I don't know one child with a full time job and children.
—Bill Hicks

If work were good for you, the rich would leave none for the poor.
—Haitian proverb

Work is of two kinds: first, altering the position of matter at or near the earth's surface relative to other matter; second, telling other people to do so.
—Bertrand Russell

Hard work never killed anybody, but why take a chance?
—Charlie McCarthy (Edgar Bergen)

Query: how to combine belief that the world is to a great extent illusory with belief that it is nonetheless essential to improve the illusion? How to be simultaneously dispassionate like an old man and active like a young one?
—Aldous Huxley, *Eyeless in Gaza*

Principally as a result of shorter vacations and fewer national holidays, the average manufacturing employee in America puts in the equivalent of eight weeks a year more at the workplace than a manufacturing employee in France or Germany.

 Thanks to all that hard work, America as a nation produces twice the goods and services per person that it produced in 1948. Everyone in the country could, in principle at least, work a four-hour day or a six-month year and still maintain a standard of living equivalent to that enjoyed by our parents. Almost uniquely among the developed nations, America took none of its productivity gains in additional leisure. It bought consumer items instead.
—Bill Bryson, *Made in America*

Hunting and gathering gave ample food supplies with far less effort than most systems of cultivation have subsequently demanded, and the switch from the carefree and lazy existence of the hunter-gatherers to the artificial and careworn life of agriculturalists requires a strong explanation. Human beings were seduced into cultivation, because at first it was easy.
—Nigel Calder, *Timescale*

The concept of time in those days was quite different from our own: for example, the notion of a mathematically regular passage of time was not accepted. Temporal duration had been closer to the old organic ideas, deriving concreteness more from the natural rhythms of the human body, the seasons, or the heavenly cycles, than from precision clockwork.
—Paul Davies, *Other Worlds*

Our ancient ancestors faced stresses far more menacing than most of us do today, of course. Few of us worry about acute starvation, being overcome by the elements, or attacks by wild beasts. Still, for this most social of social species, the constant stresses of being part of a huge, anonymous society can produce a low-grade, constant stress that our ancestors never knew. Numerous studies have shown that the most important factors in reducing stress include being among loved ones and family, and having the time for peaceful contemplation—a description much more fitting our ancestors than ourselves.
—William Allman, *The Stone Age Present*

This is the real secret of life - to be completely engaged with what you are doing in the here and now. And instead of calling it work, realize it is play.
—Alan Watts

We should have been called *Homo dissatisfactens*. From *Homo habilis* (Tool-making man) to the Sharper Image, we have been trying—unsuccessfully, it appears—to make ourselves comfortable for the last 350,000 years or so. Only a tribe of aborigines in Australia was hip enough to notice that the more one has, the shorter it feels. So they got off the treadmill when their tool count had risen to a total of five (counting the digeridoo).
—John Perry Barlow, *Wired Scenarios: The Future of the Future 1.01*

[Oscar] Wilde admires "the great aristocratic art of doing absolutely nothing"; he declares "cultivated leisure" to be "the aim of man." His target is partly the century's bustling work ethic: "Work is the curse of the drinking classes." But more importantly, he continues the Romantic withdrawal from masculine action.
—Camile Paglia, *Sexual Personae*

What happens to people who start life each morning with a small shock of alarm from their so aptly named alarm clock? Every day they become a little more conditioned to violence, and a little less accustomed to delight. Believe me, people's characteristics are decided by their mornings.
—Milan Kundera, *The Farewell Party*

Working yourself to death is a highly regarded form of suicide.
—Frans Hiddema

"That they have no ambition, that they refuse to work?!! And you consider these failings? Hombre, don't you realize that this 'ambition' that you praise is the greatest motivating evil the world has known. One must have principles *or* ambition, as these two forces are instinctive enemies and are constantly at each other's throats. Woe on the man who has both, for he will have a raging turmoil inside his person. For ambition, in the modern sense of the word, is the desire to 'get ahead,' and it is a rare man who can 'get ahead' without sacrificing his integrity and his principles. And this other thing that you consider a fault: the refusal to work in some hated job that the *payo* [non-gypsy] takes merely to make money, or gain prestige, or 'get ahead' or what have you. This rejection of work is the greatest of gypsy virtues!"
—D.E. Pohren, *The Art of Flamenco*

Robert Reich, the former secretary of labor, argues in *The Future of Success* (2001) that people for the foreseeable future need to make a choice—they can have a good job or they can have a good life.

Slackers are precisely those who argue that the good life is better than the good job...Slackers represent our fondest fantasies and our deepest fears.
—Tom Lutz, *Doing Nothing*

The Idler who habituates himself to be satisfied with what he can easily obtain, not only escapes labours which are often fruitless, but sometimes succeeds better than those who despite all that is within their reach, and think of everything more valuable as it is harder to be acquired.
—Samuel Johnson, *The Idler*

I like work; it fascinates me. I can sit and look at it for hours.
—Jerome K. Jerome

In a world where no one is compelled to work more than four hours a day, every person possessed of scientific curiosity will be able to indulge it, and every painter will be able to paint without starving, however excellent his pictures may be.
—Bertrand Russell

Find a job you like and you add five days to every week.
—H. Jackson Brown, Jr.

Divide your movements into easy-to-do sections. If you fail, divide again.
—Peter Nivio Zarlenga

The gods had condemned Sisyphus to ceaselessly rolling a rock to the top of a mountain, whence the stone would fall back of its own weight. They had thought with some reason that there is no more dreadful punishment than futile and hopeless labor.
—Albert Camus, *The Myth of Sisyphus*

Normal is getting dressed in clothes that you buy for work and driving through traffic in a car that you are still paying for—in order to get to the job you need to pay for the clothes and the car, and the house you leave vacant all day so you can afford to live in it.
—Ellen Goodman

To get the whole world out of bed
And washed, and dressed, and warmed, and fed,
To work, and back to bed again,
Believe me, Saul, costs worlds of pain.
—John Edward Masefield, *"The Everlasting Mercy"*

The best things in life are nearest: Breath in your nostrils, light in your eyes, flowers at your feet, duties at your hand, the path of right just before you. Then do not grasp at the stars, but do life's plain, common work as it comes, certain that daily duties and daily bread are the sweetest things in life.
—Robert Louis Stevenson

Things are frequently what they seem,
This is Wisdom's crown,
Whilst the game fish swims upstream,
The sensible fish swims down.
—Ogden Nash, *"When You Say That, Smile! or All Right Then, Don't Smile"*

A Lot of Strands

KEEP MY MIND LIMBER

Intellect and Uptight Thinking

There once was a time when intellectuality was a virtue. I shit you not.

Of course, this may be hard to believe in an age when bookstores have nearly all gone out of business, science is feared and untrusted, popular politicians can't spell basic words, and teachers are paid less than the custodial staff at their universities. The reasons for this descent are complex, but there may be hope on the horizon: Despite his seemingly bumbling nature, our limber-minded Dude is a direct descendant (if in name only) of a once-proud intellectual tradition. Might the Dude help breathe new life into "the life of the mind"[5]?

The earliest folks to self-apply the term "dude" were certainly lovers of deep thought. Well versed in poetry, art and philosophy, these late-19th century English "men of leisure" were the last in a long line of European romantics, distinguished by their love of the more subtle and sublime aspects of life than the hard-pressed masses outside the coffeehouses in which they spent the greater part of their lives.

Most of these early dudes were of the privileged castes, of course, but not all: Unlike other societies in class-conscious England, membership in their fraternity didn't require elegant pedigrees, but rather, prescient energies. This probably explains why they habitually enhanced their sensory organs with the help of opium and hashish.

By the time Oscar Wilde, arch-dude of the era, visited the States in 1882 (he likely helped introduce the very term "dude" to America), European romanticism had already taken root among the Yankee literati. But America was a place of reinvention, and so it was not long before stateside dudes adopted a more practical, outdoorsy character than that of their more fastidious English counterparts.

It was out here in the wide open pasture of 1800s American Transcendentalism—where the educated dandy got his hands dirty—that modern Dudeism was born. "Dude ranches" were renowned places where city folk could wax both ethereal and earthy at the same time. Synthesizing the best of both worlds was the ideal of their

---

[5] This phrase features in the Coen Brothers' film *Barton Fink*, which addresses the dark side of intellectuality as well, though in an utterly different manner.

romantic egalitarianism, and marked the beginning of a long cultural revolution which would give rise to jazz, the Beat Generation, rock and roll, the hippie movement, Pacific coast surfer culture, and today's freewheeling Internet frontier.

Sadly, instead of ushering in an age of enlightenment, this culture of cool has been continually capitalized upon by market forces, repeatedly reducing its romantic philosophy to mere marketing meme. Once the obligatory products are purchased, the theory now goes, all of us can be artists, geniuses and philosophers.

The result of this commercial pandering was that philosophy was no longer something you studied and practiced, but something you purchased and paraded around. Not surprisingly, admiration for the intellect plummeted. It may be hard to believe now, but there was a time when scientists and intellectuals with good vocabularies were portrayed as heroes in movies and the popular media; today they are almost always villains or fools, trumped in the end by their more muscular, well-dressed superiors or adversaries. Aside from Steve Jobs (who was beloved primarily because he made technology *easier*), intellectuals are regarded with, at the very best, mild suspicion.

Certainly, this anti-cerebral sentiment isn't just about envy or incomprehension. The 20th century was replete with big intellectual ideas that ended up becoming worthy of fear and distrust: eugenics, nuclear fission, Communism, genetic engineering, and so on. Many of these continue to threaten and new dangers are surely in the transom. But the way to fight against intellectualism's dark side isn't to retreat into a fundamentalist fantasy, but to propose a better intellectual argument.

In *The Big Lebowski* Walter Sobchak represents the darker side of intellectualism—though he's occasionally (some would say accidentally) proven correct, the big S.O.B. generally argues merely for the sake of argument and ego, the result being that his lofty conjectures boast very little connection to reality. The lighter side of intellectualism, on the other hand, the one we should choose to venerate, is represented in the film by none other than the Dude, the torch-bearer for the original Dudeism of the romantic era, before the life of the mind got co-opted by commercial cockcertainty.

In the Rock and Roll mockumentary *This is Spinal Tap*, lead bassist Nigel Tufnel saliently noted "It's such a fine line between stupid and clever." In *The Big Lebowski*, the Dude proves this assertion by sticking his toe back and forth over that line multiple times. But this doesn't make him stupid. On the contrary—it is his willingness and facility to err that makes him so preternaturally perceptive—by continually dabbling with the incidental ideas that come his way, maintaining a skeptical attitude, and keeping his mind resolutely "limber" that he emerges as the more sagacious and spot-on than the movie's multifarious windbags, fakers and fascists.

Walter may quote literature more effectively, but for no good reason: he always does so apropos of nothing, merely to show off. The bombastic old Big Lebowski may appear to be a brilliant businessman, but in the end he's revealed to be a fraud and a failure. Maude evinces a flawless vocabulary and cosmopolitan savvy, but she's so far up her own "strongly commended" artistic ass she can't even begin to apprehend what's really going on around her.

Against this environment, the Dude is revealed as an unrivalled genius: Though he badly misquotes Lenin (it was Cicero), he gets the gist exactly right: "see who benefits" foreshadows the key to the entire caper. His career path may be far more modest than The Big Lebowski's, but he's far more adept at the things he sets out to do. And though he often stumbles when trying to speak, he learns new words and expressions all the time because, unlike Maude, he "fucking listens occasionally."

Many people assume the "Dude" persona celebrates a sort of brain-dead modality, but his stoned behavior is only a smokescreen. Even in their dumbest incarnations (e.g. Jeff Spicoli in *Fast Times at Ridgemont High,* Bill and Ted in *Bill and Ted's Excellent Adventure* and Wayne Campbell in *Wayne's World*), righteous dudes skate between smart and simple with relative ease, and in doing so, win over both the hearts and minds of their audiences. This complementary double-aspect neatly honors the archetypal twin influences of Dudeism: café-dweller and cowpoke. It's got that whole yin-yang thing going on.

Let's not split heirs here: We need both our brains and our balls to make it to the finals. Yet without our brains, our balls are bound straight for the gutter.

There are no bigger secrets because the moment a secret is revealed, it seems little. There is only an empty secret, that keeps slipping through your fingers. Initiation is learning never to stop. The universe is peeled like an onion, and an onion is all peel.
—Umberto Eco, *Foucault's Pendulum*

That simplicity is the ultimate sophistication. What we meant by that was when you start looking at a problem and it seems really simple, with simple solutions, you don't really understand the complexity of the problem. Your solutions are way over-simplified. Then you get into the problem, and you see that it's really complicated, and you come up with all these convoluted solutions. That's sort of the middle, and that's where most people stop, and the solutions tend to work for a while. But the really great person will keep on going and find the key, the underlying principle of the problem. And come up with an elegant, really beautiful solution that works.
—Steve Jobs, quoted in *Insanely Great,* by Steven Levy

The worst-tempered people I have ever met are those who knew that they were wrong.
—David Letterman

We all do no end of feeling, and we mistake it for thinking.
—Mark Twain

The world is full of magical things patiently waiting for our wits to grow sharper.
—Bertrand Russell

The wise man doesn't give the right answers, he poses the right questions.
—Claude Levi Strauss

What feels right in ethics has a long genetic history. What feels wrong has at least as long a history in the gene lines. This gives our moral claims an intuitive sense of self evidence and a license for self deception. But our emotions arbitrate nothing. They just show that our endocrine systems work.
—Bart Kosco, *Fuzzy Thinking*

The man who views the world at fifty the same as he did at twenty has wasted thirty years of his life.
—Muhammad Ali

What the world needs is more geniuses with humility. There are so few of us left.
—Oscar Levant

"Pascal said that the heart has its reasons that reason takes no account of. If he meant what I think, he meant that when passion seizes the heart it invents reasons that seem not only plausible but conclusive to prove that the world is well lost for love. It convinces you that honour is well-sacrificed and that shame is a cheap price to pay. Passion is destructive."
—from Somerset Maugham's, *The Razor's Edge*

Mu means "no thing." Like "Quality" it points outside the process of dualistic discrimination. It states that the context of the question is such that a yes or no answer is in error and should not be given. "Unask the question" is what it says.
    When the Zen monk Joshu was asked whether a dog had a Buddha nature, he said "mu," meaning that if he answered either way he was answering incorrectly. The Buddha nature cannot be captured by yes or no questions.
—Robert Pirsig, *Zen and the art of Motorcycle Maintenance*

You don't create your own reality; psychotics create their own reality.
—Ken Wilber, *A Brief History of Everything*

We cannot reason ourselves out of our basic irrationality. All we can do is learn the art of being irrational in a reasonable way.
—Aldous Huxley, *Island*

Wit lies in recognizing the resemblance among things that differ and the difference between things that are alike.
—Anne Louise Germaine de Staël

The road to wisdom?
Well, it's plain and simple to express:
Err and err and err again
but less and less and less.
—Piet Hein

Think left and think right and think low and think high. Oh, the thinks you can think up if only you try!
—Theodor Geisel (Dr. Seuss)

The human race had always been intelligent, but from now on [the axial age] man would exercise his mind simply for the pleasure of it. These four men [progenitors of the age] were Confucius in China, Gautama (Buddha) in India, Zarathustra in Persia, and Pythagoras in Greece: four gigantic minds but four modest men, whose habits we know to have been frugal, wisdom being inimical to all passion and excess.
—Maguelonne Toussaint-Samat, *History of Food*

Better a witty fool than a foolish wit.
—William Shakespeare, *Twelfth Night*

The habit of calculated deception is common in mankind, occasional in chimpanzees, rare in baboons and virtually unknown in other animals. Deceiving and detecting deception would then be the primary reason for intelligence. They suggest that the great apes acquired a unique ability to imagine alternative possible worlds as a means to deception.
   Robert Trivers has argued that to deceive others well, an animal must deceive itself, and that self-deception's hallmark is a biased system of transfer from the conscious to the unconscious mind. Deception is therefore the reason for the invention of the *sub*conscious.
—Matt Ridley, *The Red Queen*

And when I imposed this Idea over the events of my existence—as one generally does impose one's ideas—those events—as they generally do—were forced to fall into line with the Idea which, therefore, seemed to explain everything to perfection.
—Andrew Klavan, *True Crime*

It is important to *unthink* at least once a day, for the very preservation of intellectual life.
—Alan Watts, *Om: Creative Meditation*

It's such a fine line between stupid and clever.
—Nigel Tufnel, *This is Spinal Tap (1984)*. Screenplay by Christopher Guest, Michael McKean, Harry Shearer and Rob Reiner

"I only meant to indicate the difficulty I really find in distinguishing between stupidity and cleverness. It is so hard to draw a line—one goes over into the other."
—Thomas Mann, *The Magic Mountain*

Is That What This Is?

A LOT OF INS AND OUTS

Open-mindedness and Creativity

So, we've established that the Dude is a smart feller. However, the key to the Dude's intelligence is not only book-learning—his bungalow is certainly festooned with books—but also free-thinking. In fact his mind is so limber it can sometimes be mistaken for limp, however it can stand at full attention when it needs to. Luckily for the Dude, his unfettered lifestyle ensures that isn't very often necessary.

Some who have delved deeply into *The Big Lebowski* have noted that the entire film is in many ways a pastiche of one person's experience—bits and pieces in the background of one scene will come to the foreground of Dude's consciousness. Scissors in Maude's studio will reappear in nihilist threats to cut off his "chonsson," and then become gigantic and menacing in a drug-induced dream; the loss of his Persian rug becomes conflated with neighboring Iraq's "crossing the line" into another neighbor, Kuwait. And after a toe slips over the line during a bowling tournament, another is chopped off. It seems that the Dude might have some boundary issues, probably precipitated by the fact that uninvited guests keep breaking into his house. In some ways, it might be argued, he is "fashioning" his own reality via his creative perception of the world.

One of the books clearly visible on Dude's bedroom table is Jean-Paul Sartre's *Being and Nothingness*, a work often credited as the cornerstone of existentialism, a philosophy which contends that what we call "reality" arises from our own consciousness. This might hold the key to explaining why at one point in the film Walter pointlessly exclaims "If you will it, Dude, it is no dream." Walter was quoting Theodore Hertzl's manifesto for the creation of Israel, not Sartre, but the message is almost identical.

Near the end of the film, when asked by Maude what he does for recreation, Dude replies, "Oh, the usual. Bowl. Drive around. The occasional acid flashback." As in *The Wizard of Oz*, one might wonder whether the entire story wasn't just one big dream. Note that Walter's Dog is the same as Dorothy's Toto—a Yorkie, not a Pomeranian.

And yet might it not be said that every character in the film is dreaming their own particular story? None of them, in fact, are "real." Almost all of them have donned phony masks of their own design. Moreover, after drifting through an adventure in which nothing and no one is what they seem, the Dude's limber perception of reality is the only thing he (and we, by proxy) can believe in. This is underscored in an almost Cartesian closing line: "The Dude Abides" is not that different from "I think therefore I am." Rather: *Possideo ergo sum*. I abide, therefore I am. The Dude's inertia provides the only reliable vantage point on a twirling landscape of shadows and surfaces.

In the scene just prior to this, the Dude figures out the Big Lebowski's fiction and accuses him of a crime, to which the old man replies, "You've got your story, I've got mine." It is the only honest, accurate thing the "human paraquat" says in the entire film. Yet the reason the Dude's story deserves more credence is because, like a hologram, it contains all the other characters' stories as well.

This is why the Dude's story is "so durned innarestin'," even if it is packed with wrong turns, red herrings and hallucinations. Unlike the monolithic (and false) perceptions of the others, the Dude's consciousness is multifaceted, clear and reflective as a jewel. To be "innarestin'" is the best we can expect from a world in which truth is so often frustratingly hidden and elusive. As many a wise feller has put it in one form or another, the point of life isn't about the finding of answers, but about the looking itself.

Following in the Dude's footsteps, it is incumbent upon us to make our own stories as innarestin' as possible. And the best way to do that is to keep our minds wide open. It is the modest task which is our charge—the whole durn human comedy depends on it.

In this a-here story, you're about to unfold.

Reality leaves a lot to the imagination.
—John Lennon

Everything starts as somebody's daydream.
—Larry Niven

The gift of fantasy has meant more to me than my talent for absorbing positive knowledge.
—Albert Einstein

I was trying to daydream, but my mind kept wandering.
—Stephen Wright

Te [virtue] cannot be achieved, however, until you have erased the aggressive patterns etched by society in to your nature. You must return to your natural self, to *p'u* [the "uncarved block"]. You must discard morality and ambition for if you keep these you will never be capable of compassion, moderation, and humility. When you discard some of your wishes, you will have them all.
—Holmes Welch, *Taoism: The Parting of the Way*

The creative individual has the capacity to free himself from the web of social pressures in which the rest of us are caught. He is capable of questioning the assumptions that the rest of us accept.
—John W. Gardner, *On Writers and Writing*

What is being awake if not interpreting our dreams, or dreaming if not interpreting our wake? Circle of circles!
Jonathan Safran Foer, *Everything is Illuminated*

When asked how he came to discover relativity theory, Einstein replied that he thought about how things would look if he happened to be riding along on a beam of light. What he was saying is that sometimes things look different if you're inside the system than if you look at what's happening from the outside.
—John L. Casti, *Complexification*

Do not attempt to adjust your radio. We will return it to you as soon as you are groovy.
—George Clinton, *"P. Funk (Wants To Get Funked Up)"*

If you have an apple and I have an apple and we exchange apples then you and I will still each have one apple. But if you have an idea and I have an idea and we exchange these ideas, then each of us will have two ideas.
—George Bernard Shaw

If the fool would persist in his folly he would become wise.
—William Blake, *The Proverbs of Hell*

Walker, there is no path. The path is made by walking.
—Antonio Machado

To broaden your horizon, take a step forward.
—Frans Hiddema

Do not go where the path may lead, go instead where there is no path and leave a trail.
—Ralph Waldo Emerson

The ruts are deepest in the middle of the road.
—James Richardson

They will say you are on the wrong road, if it is your own.
—Antonio Porchia

Some people think of the glass as half full. Some people think of the glass as half empty. I think of the glass as too big.
—George Carlin

To know only one thing well is to have a barbaric mind: civilization implies the graceful relation of all varieties of experience to a central humane system of thought. The present age is peculiarly barbaric…The scholar is a quarryman, not a builder, and all that is required of him is that he should quarry cleanly…[the poet's] function is truth, whereas the scholar's is fact.
—Robert Graves, *The White Goddess*

Once in a while you get shown the light in the strangest of places if you look at it right.
—Robert Hunter, "Scarlet Begonias"

I like nonsense, it wakes up the brain cells. Fantasy is a necessary ingredient in living, It's a way of looking at life through the wrong end of a telescope. Which is what I do. And that enables you to laugh at life's realities.
—Theodor Geisel (Dr. Seuss)

The most exemplary life and ideas which these centuries can offer end on a profound acknowledgement of ignorance.
—Albert Camus, *Summer*

All I know is that I know nothing.
—Socrates

The fact that an opinion has been widely held is no evidence whatever that it is not utterly absurd.
—Bertrand Russell

Whenever you find yourself on the side of the majority, it is time to pause and reflect.
—Mark Twain

Keeping an open mind is a virtue, but not so open that your brains fall out.
—James Oberg

I have never been a serious person.... I am not serious at all because existence is not serious. It is so playful, so full of song and so full of music and so full of subtle laughter. It has no purpose; it is not business-like. It is pure joy, sheer dance, out of overflowing energy.
—Bhagwan Shree Rajneesh (Osho)

It is the mark of an educated mind to be able to entertain a thought without accepting it.
—Aristotle

Drawing fine lines is a human tendency, an attempt to make our simplified mental labeling system match a differently structured world; but in that world boundaries may be fuzzy, or fractal, or may not exist at all.
—Ian Stewart and Jack Cohen, *The Collapse of Chaos*

It is easy in the world to live after the world's opinion; it is easy in solitude to live after our own; but the great man is he who in the midst of the crowd keeps with perfect sweetness the independence of solitude.
—Ralph Waldo Emerson

The trouble with the world is that the stupid are cocksure and the intelligent are full of doubt.
—Bertrand Russell

The world is like a ride in an amusement park. And when you choose to go on it you think it's real because that's how powerful our minds are. And the ride goes up and down and round and round. It has thrills and chills and it's very brightly colored and it's very loud and it's fun, for a while. Some people have been on the ride for a long time and they begin to question: "Is this real, or is this just a ride?" And other people have remembered, and they come back to us, they say, "Hey, don't worry, don't be afraid, ever, because this is just a ride." And we kill those people.
—Bill Hicks

Open-mindedness is virtually the same as morality.
—Henrik Ibsen

People who say they don't care what people think are usually desperate to have people think they don't care what people think.
—George Carlin

The test of a first-rate intelligence is the ability to hold two opposed ideas in the mind at the same time, and still retain the ability to function. One should, for example, be able to see that things are hopeless and yet be determined to make them otherwise.
—F. Scott Fitzgerald

Common sense is the collection of prejudices acquired by age eighteen.
—Albert Einstein

Talent is commonly developed at the expense of character.
—Ralph Waldo Emerson

Specialization tends to limit the field of problems that the specialist is concerned with. Now, the person who isn't a specialist, but a generalist like myself, sees something over here that he has learned from one specialist, something over there that he has learned from another specialist—and neither of them has considered the problem of why this occurs here and also there. So the generalist gets into a range of other problems that are more genuinely human, you might say, than specifically cultural.
—Joseph Campbell, *The Power of Myth*

I never set out to be weird. It was always other people who called me weird.
—Frank Zappa

Hipkat, the [African] Wolof word denoting a person who is attuned to his environment, literally "has his eyes open," is the most plausible source for *hepcat* and *hip* and their many variants.
—Bill Bryson, *Made in America*

The positive thing about the skeptic is that he considers everything possible.
—Thomas Mann

To use your head, you have to go out of your mind.
—Timothy Leary

The desire for order is the virtuous pretext by which man's hatred for man justifies its crimes.
—Roger Grenier, *The Difficulty of Being a Dog*

It has been written that it is easy to get the mob to agree with you—all you have to do is agree with the mob.
—David Mamet, *True and False*

Man specializes in being versatile. Human genes specify the character of *versatility*.
—Ian Stewart and Jack Cohen, *The Collapse of Chaos*

Fear is the main source of superstition, and one of the main sources of cruelty. To conquer fear is the beginning of wisdom.
—Bertrand Russell

Most people are other people. Their thoughts are someone else's opinions, their lives a mimicry, their passions a quotation.
—Oscar Wilde

As you open your awareness, life will improve of itself, you won't even have to try. It's a beautiful paradox: the more you open your consciousness, the fewer unpleasant events intrude themselves into your awareness.
—Thaddeus Golas

Pluralism and Tolerance - 83

Abide Another

THAT'S JUST, LIKE, UH, YOUR OPINION, MAN

Pluralism and Tolerance

Despite all the quaint retro rhetoric about the United States being a melting pot culture, where people and ideas from various backgrounds freely intermingle, in truth the country resembles not so much a melting pot as it does an early-bird buffet. That is, though there's lots of stuff on offer, most people are rather picky about what they put on their plate. Our vaunted multiculturalism consists largely of Italian pizza, French fries, and music which originated in Africa and Ireland.

In all fairness to America, though, most of the rest of the world is the same, or worse. Folks just don't dig each other's style.

On the bright side, tolerance has progressed greatly over the centuries. Many ancient cultures had the same word for "stranger" as they did for "enemy," which explains why "travel" and "travail" are also the same word. "Hanging out" with the locals often meant exactly that—from a tree. Ever thus to offbeats.

Los Angeles, where *The Big Lebowski* is set, is a good example of a melting pot society in which it's possible for people to hate each other and still kind of get along. On one hand, the massive urban sprawl keeps groups of people apart, but at the same time its charms draw people inexorably in a never-ending attempt to fill the gaps: Its role as pop culture Mecca, its location at the end of the great cultural push westward, and its bastion of the best weather in the country ensure that every kind of nutjob on Earth passes through its hurly-burly pearly gates. It's as if the country was tilted and those without roots had no choice but to roll that way. The result is that L.A. is both highly diverse and tolerant, and at the same time comfortably ignorant of its own diversity and tolerance. Thus, a racist bigot is just another goddamn moron to point at and ridicule, just as he does towards others. It kind of works.

Though quirky, the characters in *The Big Lebowski* are not all that different from the folks you'd encounter in Los Angeles if you wandered around a bit. Then again, no one really wanders because everyone gets around by car. Except when shopping and giving each other the finger on the freeway, people don't interact much.

There are exceptions. On the boardwalk of the funky little enclave of Venice beach, for instance, near where the Dude lived, everyone from artists to businessmen to jocks to the mentally ill rubs casually-clad elbows every day.

It is not by accident that the Dude lived there—nowhere else in Los Angeles can one find such a motley mishmash of mankind. Here, at the furthest end of the great western expansion of civilization, America has produced the greatest realization of the vaunted melting pot idea—where everything is bubbling, ridiculous, half-baked, and overcooked in equal measure.

Though personal freedom on Venice beach has been cracked down upon recently, this was once the most welcoming zootopia on the planet—despite its superior reputation as a freedom freakshow, the Haight/Ashbury area of San Francisco was actually ugly, violent and cold-hearted in comparison. And where the Haight fell apart after the 'sixties, Venice remained relatively hip until the turn of the millennium, after which the funky free spirit began to be curtailed largely as a result of soaring real estate prices.

As the Stranger intones at the outset, the Dude was the "man for his time and place." Of all the characters in the film, the Dude is the only one who could rightfully claim to be tolerant to any significant degree. Every other character, from The Big Lebowski to Walter to The Jesus, and even most of the minor characters, are defined by their petty prejudices and bloated sense of self-righteousness. The very title of this chapter is hilariously uttered by the Dude after the Jesus lambasts him mercilessly—not a typical reaction by any stretch. When someone says they're "going to fuck you up" and you reply "that's just, like, your opinion, man" then it's not likely that opinions are something you are terribly precious about.

This is hardly a typical red-blooded American male point of view, and precisely what makes the Dude superlatively tolerant of other folks' foibles. Against the backdrop of an ill-advised escapade in the Persian Gulf, the Dude emerges as the ultimate conscientious objector. Other than offhandedly calling him a "creep" while simultaneously complimenting his bowling skill, the Dude doesn't express a shred of disdain for The Jesus, one of the most absurdly offensive characters in modern comedic film. Nor does he remain angry for long at The Big Lebowski after being mercilessly taunted by him, nor again later after he discovers his evil plan to rob underprivileged children. Over and over again in the course of the film the Dude gets beaten and mistreated and yet never finds it in his heart to openly despise anyone.

In fact, the Dude's continual recourse to "turn the other cheek" and not judge others brings to mind the original biblical Jesus. Could it be that "That's just, like, uh, your opinion, man" is just a fuzzy-headed reworking of the Nazarene Jesus' "Judge not, that you not be judged?" Not to mention the haircut, beard, sandals and the flowing robe.

It wasn't a coincidence that Christianity and other similarly pluralistic, tolerant doctrines (Buddhism, Jainism, Taoism, Epicureanism) arose at roughly the same time all over the world. These doctrines, much more accepting than their forebears

(Judaism, Hinduism, Confucianism) came about primarily to deal with the fact that disparate peoples were suddenly living much closer together as a result of the agricultural revolution and the rise of cities. Suddenly, everyone had to work together in bigger groups to farm and protect territory and grain stores. Before large-scale agriculture got off the ground, humans lived in tight-knit kin groups of only about one hundred to two hundred people. They didn't need to, and couldn't really afford to be, very tolerant or trusting of strangers.

Whereas for eons people had been accustomed to identify with their ethnicities and mother tongues, these so-called "Axial age" philosophies helped bring people together with their own variations of the "golden rule": Do unto others as you would have them to unto you, even if they're fucking perverts. To some degree, it worked—civilization as we know it would have been impossible otherwise. But we still have a long way to go. Most citizens of Earth are nowhere near living up to that ideal, still hardwired with distrust and hatred from many outdated eons ago.

As noted above, Los Angeles marks the final physical frontier of the Western expansion, and to some degree, the edge of its philosophical tradition. If indeed the Dude is "the man for his time and place" as the narrator of the film indicates, it is at least partially because he alone represents the greatest hope of western civilization: that we might one day be truly *civil* to one another.

Think for yourselves and let others enjoy the privilege to do so, too.
—Voltaire

It is well to remember that the entire universe, with one trifling exception, is composed of others.
—John Andrew Holmes

To be yourself in a world that is constantly trying to make you something else is the greatest accomplishment.
—Ralph Waldo Emerson

Nobody realizes that some people expend tremendous energy merely to be normal.
—Albert Camus

I'm the one that has to die when it's time for me to die, so let me live my life, the way I want to.
—Jimi Hendrix

Undisturbed calmness of mind is attained by cultivating friendliness toward the happy, compassion for the unhappy, delight in the virtuous, and indifference toward the wicked.
—Christopher Isherwood, *How To Know God: Patanjali's Yoga Sutras*

Prejudices are what fools use for reason.
—Voltaire

For all his tattooing he was on the whole a clean, comely looking cannibal...Better sleep with a sober cannibal than a drunken Christian.
—Herman Melville, *Moby Dick*

There's nothing worse than a yellow-bellied freak, unless that's his act.
—Concert manager, *The Simpsons*, season 7, episode 24. Script by Brent Forrester

Everybody is ignorant. Only on different subjects.
—Will Rogers

Nonconformists travel as a rule in bunches. You rarely find a nonconformist who goes it alone. And woe to him inside a nonconformist clique who does not conform with nonconformity.
—Eric Hoffer, *Reflections on the Human Condition*

A global perspective is not innate; the infant is not born with it; hominids did not possess it. A global perspective is a rare, elite, extraordinary perspective of great depth, and there are relatively few individuals who actually make it to that depth.
—Ken Wilber, *A Brief History of Everything*

One should respect public opinion insofar as is necessary to avoid starvation and keep out of prison, but anything that goes beyond this is voluntary submission to an unnecessary tyranny.
—Bertrand Russell

I don't like that man. I must get to know him better.
—Abraham Lincoln

If cultures are only individuals writ large, as Salman Rushdie and Gabriel Garcia Marquez have suggested, individuals are small cultures in themselves.
—Pico Iyer, *Video Night in Kathmandu*

Be humble for you are made of dung. Be noble for you are made of stars.
—*Serbian Proverb*

One of the most potent divisive factors is the claim to complete or absolute truth, whether of revelation, dogma, righteousness, or anything else. Systems based on any such absolute inevitability come up against new facts and discoveries which are in opposition to their pretensions. The only method then open is to assert that the new ideas are also absolute, in the opposed sense of being absolutely wrong; and this at once creates division, and shuts the door on synthesis and development. A claim to absolute truth may be dressed up to appear as a claim to universality: but in point of fact it is always particular and not general, and can never become truly universal. *Le mieux c'est l'ennemi du bien* [The ideal is the enemy of the good].
—Julian Huxley, *New Bottles for New Wine*

The first human being who hurled an insult instead of a stone was the founder of civilization.
—Sigmund Freud

Accept the ways of others. Respect first your own.
—Master Po, *Kung Fu (1972)*, Season 1, Episode 8. Script by Halsted Welles

To have a horror of the bourgeois is bourgeois.
—Jules Renard

I have accordingly no private utopia: if I had one, it would have to include the private utopias of many other men, and the realized ideals of many other societies; for life has still too many potentialities to be encompassed by the projects of a single generation, by the hopes and beliefs of a single thinker. Unlike most utopian writers, I must find a place in any scheme for challenge and opposition and conflict, for evil and corruption, since they are visible in the natural history of all societies.
—Lewis Mumford, *The Story of Utopias*

No man is a hypocrite in his pleasures.
—Samuel Johnson

Do not fear to be eccentric in opinion, for every opinion now accepted was once eccentric.
—Bertrand Russell

The idea of hip is that you set yourself apart in terms of discrimination, intelligence and awareness from the rest of the people. But if you don't do it with a certain leavening of irony, you're going to be a preening asshole. You have to have some objectivity. If you start wearing a beret, dark glasses and a goatee, and you're serious about it, too bad for you. You have to be tongue-in-cheek and kidding on the square.
—Jerry Wexler

If you hate a person, you hate something in him that is a part of yourself. What isn't part of ourselves doesn't disturb us.
—Herman Hesse

The height of luxury: own car, own house, own opinion.
—Wieslaw Brudzinski

I think we ought always to entertain our opinions with some measure of doubt. I shouldn't wish people dogmatically to believe any philosophy, not even mine.
—Bertrand Russell

I can't stand in judgment of you…I'm not perfect…yet.
—Angus MacGyver, *MacGyver*, Season 1, episode 7. Script by Judy Burns

You Know Me, I Can't Complain

CAN'T BE WORRIED ABOUT THAT SHIT

Peace of Mind

The Big Lebowski isn't just a comedy. It's also a commentary on "the whole durn human comedy," as The Stranger calls it. Fancy embellishments aside, the history of human thought may be summed up in this single sentence: *Why aren't we happy, and is there any way we can be?* Like the Dude, just when we think everything is tied together, the rug gets pulled out from under us.

For a long time, western religion was convinced that unhappiness was the result of our exile from paradise. On the other side of the planet, eastern religions claimed it came from laboring under illusions about the nature of reality.

These ideas remained pretty much unchallenged until the intellectual revolutions of the 1500s and 1600s, after which Enlightenment philosophers decided that happiness could gradually be engineered by science and social engineering.

When that didn't pan out, the Romantic philosophers blamed society for our misery, lobbying instead for half-baked anarchy or pie-in-the-sky Utopias.

Following this, capitalism and socialism both rushed in to fill the void, claiming happiness grew from wealth and work, and differed only about the best way to distribute the benefits. It didn't matter, though, because the masses under both systems remained stubbornly discontent.

Finally, in the mid-20th century academic post-modernism jumped in and claimed that since happiness was based on power, and that since power was corruptive and inherently unfair, no one could ever be happy, not even the powerful.

While ivory tower academics appeared content with this deterministic detente, under their noses consumerism had become the *de facto* way forward for most folks, businesses everywhere selling little bits of temporary glee in cheerful plastic packaging. Though happiness still couldn't be secured, it seemed that an endless army of amusements could at least distract us from boredom and despair. This is where we still are today.

That's more or less the history of happiness. Westward the woebegones. That about wraps up why we feel down.

But wait! Recently, however, another peace-of-mind puzzle piece has emerged: *evolutionary psychology*. In fact, this relatively new worldview has increasingly provided the basis of emerging academic theories, much the way postmodernism did up to the end of last century.

The far out thing is, for the first time, it all actually kind of makes sense.

Evolutionary psychology argues that we were actually pretty content once, about 100,000 years ago when we lived in groups of about 100-150 people on the African savannah. There was plenty of food, the weather was good, and the only thing to worry about was big cats, fleas, and typical small-town gossip.

We lived for so long in that stable environment (maybe 80,000 years), that our brains adapted evolutionarily to that lifestyle and setting and the psychological notion that this was "normal" became written into our genes.

Then everything changed. About 20,000 years ago the weather shifted dramatically, food got scarce, violence got more common, and we all got bummed out. Since then, our surroundings have continued to change so much and so rapidly that we haven't had a chance to properly adapt to it. Genetic evolution is a tediously slow process after all: down through the generations, across the genetic strands of time.

Luckily, our noodles are as flexible as fettuccine, and given the right mental programming hacks we can make the best of a bad situation. In the Dude's case, the hack is to try and make his Stone Age brain feel right at home. Gotta feed the monkey.

In many ways the Dude has recreated in his own life a workable analogue of life on the African savannah: he owns little of value, has a loyal, intimate set of friends, a good number of steadfast acquaintances (most bowling leagues contain 100-150 members), lives in a place known for its pleasingly warm weather, and spends plenty of time "taking it easy," which is exactly what people did for the majority of their lives all those eons ago. Furthermore, there were no nuclear families back then—the group raised the children together, so monogamy and complex familial obligations were rare. And though portraits from 100,000 years ago are hard to come by, he probably even wears his hair the same way they did.

Oh, also, according to the fossil record, it seems there may have been a lot of freely-available, unregulated dope.

Aside from recreating a paradise lost, the Dude also employs the Dudeist teachings of the more civilized ages to help him get through the day. Most of this wisdom is just footnotes to Lao Tzu and Epicurus, but the general message is this: down deep, your brain knows what's really important in life. You just have to spend a lot of time getting deep to access the mines of information.

Just as the Dude chides the hyper-intellectual brain of ultra-modern Maude, "Why don't you fucking listen occasionally? You might learn something" he could also mean that everything we need is right in front of us, but for the fact that our thinking about everything has become so uptight. What the strands in our stone-age heads are saying to us might well be an echo of Walter Sobchak's indignant refrain: 100,000 years of beautiful tradition? You're goddamn right we're living in the past!

The happiest years go by and we fail to recognize them for what they are. They are obscured by petty annoyances, present anxieties, or dreams for the future.
—Carobeth Laird, *Encounter with an Angry God*

You probably wouldn't worry about what people think of you if you could know how seldom they do.
—Olin Miller

And which of you by being anxious can add one cubit to his span of life?
—Jesus Christ, *Luke 12:25*

I may be crazy, but it keeps me from going insane.
—Waylon Jennings

If I had no sense of humor, I would long ago have committed suicide.
—Mahatma Gandhi

What fates impose, that men must needs abide
It boots not to resist both wind and tide.
—William Shakespeare

Only the just man enjoys peace of mind.
—Epicurus

Therefore do not worry about tomorrow, for tomorrow will worry about itself. Each day has enough trouble of its own.
—Jesus Christ, *Matthew 6:34*

Only when we are sick of our sickness
Shall we cease to be sick.
—Lao Tzu, *The Tao Te Ching,* translated by John C. H. Wu

I think I've discovered the secret of life—you just hang around until you get used to it.
—Charles M. Schulz

If you think you have it tough, read history books.
—Bill Maher

If you want to make a man happy, don't add to his riches, but subtract from his desires.
—Epicurus

The hardest arithmetic to master is that which enables us to count our blessings.
—Eric Hoffer, *Reflections on the Human Condition*

It's a troublesome world. All the people who're in it
Are troubled with troubles almost every minute.
You ought to be thankful, a whole heaping lot,
For the places and people you're lucky you're not.
—Theodor Geisel (Dr. Seuss)

When life gives you lemons…just say "fuck the lemons" and bail!
—Chuck, *Forgetting Sarah Marshall (2008)*, screenplay by Jason Segel

Light-hearted people take serious things lightly and light things seriously.
—Maria de Beausacq

Hope for the best
Expect the worst
Life's a play.
We're unrehearsed.
—Mel Brooks

That the birds of worry and care fly above your head, this you cannot change. But that they build nests in your hair, this you can prevent.
—*Chinese Proverb*

Muddy water is best cleared by leaving it alone.
—Alan Watts

A man must be able to cut a knot, for everything cannot be untied; he must know how to disengage what is essential from the detail in which it is enwrapped, for not everything can be equally considered; in a word, he must be able to simplify his duties, his business, and his life.
—Henri Frédéric Amiel

Make friends with yourself completely, without hesitations, without false modesty, without fears and without hopes.
—Federico Fellini

My opinion is that you never find happiness until you stop looking for it.
—Chuang Tzu

No one can make you feel inferior without your consent.
—Eleanor Roosevelt

When you are sorrowful look again in your heart,
And you shall see that in truth you are weeping
For that which has been your delight.
—Kahlil Gibran, *The Prophet*

Most folks are as happy as they make up their minds to be.
—Abraham Lincoln

Is life worth living?
Aye, with the best of us,
Heights of us, depths of us—
Life is the test of us!
—Corinne Roosevelt Robinson, *"Life, A Question?"*

We want happy paintings. Happy paintings. If you want sad things, watch the news.
—Bob Ross, *The Joy of Painting*

It is not how old you are, but how you are old.
—Jules Renard

Oh, of course everything looks bad if you remember it.
—Homer Simpson, *The Simpsons*, Season 8, Episode 9, script by Ken Keeler

Any idiot can face a crisis. It is this day-to-day living that wears you out.
—Anton Chekov

Do what you can to do what you ought, and leave hoping and fearing alone.
—T.H. Huxley, *Science and Education*

We are no longer happy as soon as we wish to be happier.
—Walter Savage Landor

Life is thickly sown with thorns, and I know no other remedy than to pass quickly through them. The longer we dwell on our misfortunes, the greater is their power to harm us.
—Voltaire

Happiness cannot be pursued; it can only ensue.
—Viktor E. Frankl, *Man's Search for Meaning*

I, not events, have the power to make me happy or unhappy today. I can choose which it shall be. Yesterday is dead, tomorrow hasn't arrived yet. I have just one day, today, and I'm going to be happy in it.
—Groucho Marx

A light heart lives long.
—William Shakespeare, *Love's Labour's Lost*

You are no bigger than the things that annoy you.
—Jerry Bundsen

It's only possible to live happily ever after on a day to day basis.
—Margaret Bonnano

Nothing is as ridiculous as the fear of being ridiculous.
—Tadeusz Gicgier

Don't cry because it's over. Smile because it happened.
—Theodor Geisel (Dr. Seuss)

The philosopher is nature's pilot. And there you have our difference; to be in Hell is to drift: to be in Heaven is to steer.
—George Bernard Shaw, *Man and Superman*

The waist is a terrible thing to mind.
—Tom Wilson, *Ziggy*

Care about people's approval
And you become their prisoner.
—Lao Tzu, *The Tao Te Ching,* translated by Stephen Mitchell

There is no cure for birth and death save to enjoy the interval.
—George Santayana, *Soliloquies in England*

Don't sweat the petty things and don't pet the sweaty things.
—George Carlin

Frustration is an experience we cannot dodge. Fashionable as it is to think that none of us can be happy until we fulfill our potential, fulfilling our potential to its limit is an absolute impossibility. If a bacterium were allowed to fulfill its potential, within only four days it could produce more progeny than there are protons in the universe. Fortunately, reality's constraints have kept bacteria from acting out their full reproductive possibilities.
—Howard Bloom, *The Lucifer Principle*

I wish you a good day, which is no mean accomplishment.
—Arthur Rimbaud

Don't waste your time on jealousy. Sometimes you're ahead, sometimes you're behind. The race is long and, in the end, it's only with yourself.
—Mary Schmich, *Wear Sunscreen*

The last of human freedoms is the ability to choose one's attitude in a given set of circumstances. This ultimate freedom was recognized by the ancient Stoics as well as by modern existentialists.
—Viktor E. Frankl, *Man's Search for Meaning,*

Emotion, which is suffering, ceases to be suffering as soon as we form a clear and precise picture of it.
—Spinoza, *Ethics*

The mind is its own place, and in it self
Can make a Heav'n of Hell, a Hell of Heav'n
—John Milton, *Paradise Lost*

"I'm scared of things I don't understand."
"Then you must be frightened a great deal."
—Graham Greene, *A Burnt-Out Case*

Lao Tzu has an important message. He does not tell [the disenfranchised] that they have an immortal soul which an infinitely just God may one day reward with millennial splendor for their present obscurity. Rather, he tells them that they are wise to be obscure...that this unbearable stone which they have thought they must push to the top of the hill may be discarded.
—Holmes Welch, *Taoism: The Parting of the Way*

Eight Miles High

AND PROUD WE ARE OF ALL OF THEM

Ambition and Achievement

Though most toilet stall philosophy tends to be sexual or scatological in nature, the occasional lofty observation gets scribbled down now and then, much to the delight of the perceptive pooper. This one is among the best:

"To do is to be."—Socrates
"To be is to do."—Sartre
"Do-be-do-be-do"—Sinatra

What makes this bit of bathroom bathos so absorbing is that it first digests the big questions about doing and being, and then dumps the words like the empty vehicles they are. Thus "do" and "be" are not so different from doo and pee.

When confronted with the issue of action and ambition, Taoism counsels *wu wei*, or "inactive action" instead. As we've mentioned in the chapter on Taoism, *wu wei* is practiced by acting naturally, not aggressively. One proceeds without dwelling upon the result or even the action itself—rather, one simply moves as the situation dictates. To resist, or to push too hard reduces the effectiveness and appropriateness of the action. It certainly takes talent to employ *wu wei* effectively—even a skilled Taoist like the Dude repeatedly got it wrong.

As stated previously, the Coen Brothers may well have had *wu wei* in mind when they started the movie by having Woo, a "Chinaman" wee upon the Dude's rug. Urinating, in fact, is the most perfect example of "doing by not doing." Just letting things flow.

What's more, water is the metaphor most relied upon in the Tao Te Ching. According to several of the book's verses, water's flow is subtle but steady, wearing away at strong things without force, powerful because it flows in low places men reject. It is both the humblest and most important thing on earth. Like the Dude, it is both high and lowdown, and it follows the gravity, twists, turns and switchbacks demanded naturally by any situation.

Incidentally, water also would have been highly effective in washing the piss from the rug, and thus would have prevented all the trouble which followed. But then, of course, *The Big Lebowski* wouldn't have been much of a movie.

The Dude's "ambition"—merely to return things back to the status quo—is similar to water seeking its level, and a markedly different approach from the other characters in the film, most of whom are struggling to flow uphill, against the current, against gravity, and even possibly against their own natures. Consequently, the Dude's actions generally seem truer and turn out more effective, even if he suffers a switchback from time to time.

The Dude's favorite pastime illuminates this type of action: bowling is perhaps second only to archery in its Zen-like simplicity and elegant, single-pointed vector of movement. The Dude rolls straight through life like a yin-yang bowling ball, enjoying its slow momentum and accepting the incidental vicissitudes of rotation, spin, and the occasional gutter.

Viewers are prone to chuckle when, after sleeping with Maude, the Dude languidly shares with her his pathetic employment history. It seems that he has accomplished virtually nothing in his nearly fifty years on the planet. In contrast, Maude herself is overtly proud commendations received for painting abstract vaginas. Her father, the Big Lebowski, arrogantly touts a "life of achievement...challenges met, competitors bested, obstacles overcome." Other characters are hardly humbler: Walter is relentlessly cocky about his tour in Vietnam twenty years ago and his DIY erudition; the Jesus is a grotesque self-promoter of both his bowling skill and bulging scrotum; and even Donnie, who is otherwise virtually silent throughout the film shamelessly gloats every time he makes a strike—"You guys are dead in the water!" and "I'm throwing rocks tonight!"

But who has accomplished most by the end? The Dude. He solves the case, gets the girl (if briefly), and sacrifices none of his self-respect. He achieves everything by practicing the figurative nothingness of *wu wei*, while others are running around making a big deal about of a quite literal nothingness. A kidnapping and ransom caper in which there was neither a kidnapping nor a ransom? Sounds like another Zen koan:

Student: Master, how may one kidnap themselves?
Master: Do whatever it takes no matter what the cost.
Student: Throw out a ringer for a ringer?
Master: That's what your parents did.

If it weren't for Walter's aggressively Confucian "giving a shit about the rules" Dude never would have gotten caught up in the whole caper in the first place. The Dude doesn't really care that much about his rug. It's only Walter's incessant prodding which impels him to lose his way, to briefly "kidnap himself" as it were.

Nevertheless, given the modest task which is his charge, he proves to be the man for his time and place, with a mind wide open, resilient, and limber enough to figure everything out. Of course, he never does get his rug back—this is the price he pays for going against the flow. When the Stranger says "sometimes you eat the bear, sometimes the bear, well, he eats you," he forgot to emphasize that one might merely leave hungry bears alone[6].

Regular attendees of "Lebowskifests"—a series of Lebowski-themed gatherings held all over the world—proudly wear T-shirts which say "ACHEIVER" on them. This is in homage to the "Little Lebowski Urban Achievers," the charity the Big Lebowski founded. But of course, after the old man embezzles a million dollars from the charity's coffers, any hopes the achievers may have had to achieve anything are greatly compromised.

Without a wealthy patron to foot the bill, the "achievers" who created Lebowskifest had to start the whole thing off on the extremely cheap, but it was, and continues to be, an inspired, affordable and truly enjoyable event. Lebowskifest was conceived as "a natural, zesty enterprise" (Maude's euphemism for humping) and like the sexual urge itself, it has developed by following an organic, self-propelling *wu wei*-style flow.

But then, that's precisely the way the whole durned human comedy keeps perpetuatin' itself. Those that practice *wu wei* often achieve even if that wasn't part of their original plan. The chances of conception are increased by doing what comes naturally, and also with a great deal of zest.

We should take comfort in that. Socrates, Sartre and even Sinatra would probably agree. Stop worrying what to *do* or what to *be*, and pass the *doobie*. With the right attitude, good things shall come to pass.

---

[6] There has been much debate over whether the Stranger says "bear" or "bar." It's bar. "Bar" is merely an olde tymey American cowboy way of saying "bear."

To dwell upon the result is to glorify something very fleeting, or even to block the way to higher attainment by aiming too low.
—Ernest Wood, *Concentration*

Nothing is enough for the man to whom enough is too little.
—Epicurus

Besides the noble art of getting things done, there is the noble art of leaving things undone. The wisdom of life consists in the elimination of non-essentials.
—Lin Yutang, *The Importance of Living*

We don't make mistakes, we make happy little accidents.
—Bob Ross, *The Joy of Painting*

I've made an odd discovery. Every time I talk to a savant I feel quite sure that happiness is no longer a possibility. Yet when I talk with my gardener, I'm convinced of the opposite.
—Bertrand Russell

If you get up one more time than you fall you will make it through.
—*Chinese proverb*

The trouble with the rat race is that even if you win, you're still a rat.
—Lily Tomlin

He who is slow to anger is better than the mighty,
And he who rules his spirit, than he who captures a city.
—*Proverbs 16:32*

I'm not miserable, I'm dissatisfied. That's what makes me a success.
—Francis Fitzpatrick, *She's the One (1996)*. Screenplay by Edward Burns

What's money? A man is a success if he gets up in the morning and gets to bed at night, and in between he does what he wants to do.
—Bob Dylan

Upon the highest throne in the world, we are seated, still, upon our asses.
—Michel de Montaigne, *The Essays*

If at first you don't succeed, try, try, and try again. Then give up. There's no use being a damned fool about it.
—W. C. Fields

Success is having to worry about every damn thing in the world, except money.
—Johnny Cash

Do not spoil what you have by desiring what you have not; remember that what you now have was once among the things you only hoped for.
—Epicurus

Don't put off for tomorrow what you can do today, because if you enjoy it today, you can do it again tomorrow.
—James Michener

Whatever you do, you should do it right. Even if it's something wrong.
—Hank Hill, *King of the Hill*, Season 1, Episode 10. Script by Jonathan Collier & Joe Stillman

[The Dude's ethos] is linked to the religion of laughter promoted by Preston Sturges in *Sullivan's Travels*...We think we ought to care about money, status, success and all the other markers of how the world sorts out its winners and losers. But, in truth, everyone knows that these are not the things that really matter. Instead, we ought to enjoy the only life that has been given to us, with its simple pleasures of play, laughter, music, games, and fellow-feeling.
—J.M. Tyree & Ben Walters, *BFI Film Classics: The Big Lebowski*

It is not life and wealth and power that enslave men, but the cleaving to life and wealth and power.
—The Buddha

Success is the ability to go from failure to failure with no loss of enthusiasm.
—Winston Churchill

Some run after good fortune not realizing that good fortune is running after them, but never reaches them, because they are running.
—Bert Hellinger

Sometimes I wonder whether the world is being run by smart people who are putting us on or by imbeciles who really mean it.
—Mark Twain

Anyone who is capable of getting themselves made President should on no account be allowed to do the job.
—Douglas Adams, *The Hitchhiker's Guide to the Galaxy*

My life has no purpose, no direction, no aim, no meaning, and yet I'm happy. I can't figure it out. What am I doing right?
—Snoopy, *Peanuts* by Charles M. Schulz

The meek shall inherit the earth, but not the mineral rights.
—J. Paul Getty

Basically you have to suppress your own ambitions in order to be who you need to be.
—Bob Dylan

When you're betting for tiles in an archery contest, you shoot with skill. When you're betting for fancy belt buckles, you worry about your aim. And when you're betting for real gold, you're a nervous wreck. Your skill is the same in all three cases—but because one prize means more to you than another, you let outside considerations weigh on your mind. He who looks too hard at the outside gets clumsy on the inside.
—Chuang Tzu

Great spirits have always encountered violent opposition from mediocre minds.
—Albert Einstein

The depressing thing about tennis is that no matter how good I get, I'll never be as good as a wall.
—Mitch Hedberg

There is a violence, even a guilt, inherent in the posture of greatness, of power. Kafka expresses the dream conviction that to lower one's profile is to preserve innocence and, perhaps, even to see more of the sky.
—Avivah Zornberg, *The Beginning of Desire*

Self-sufficiency is the greatest of all wealth.
—Epicurus

How does the sea become the king of all streams? Because it lies lower than they!
—Lao Tzu, *The Tao Te Ching*, translated by John C. H. Wu

For everything you have missed, you have gained something else, and for everything you gain, you lose something else.
—Ralph Waldo Emerson

If I had known they were going to do this [drop Atom Bombs on Hiroshima and Nagasaki], I would have become a watchmaker.
—Albert Einstein

The Master, by abiding in the Tao, sets an example for all beings.
Because he doesn't display himself, people can see his light.
Because he has nothing to prove, people can trust his words.
Because he doesn't know who he is,
    people recognize themselves in him.
He does not seek excellence, therefore he will be exalted.
—Lao Tzu, *The Tao Te Ching*, translated by Stephen Mitchell

One's real life is so often the life that one does not lead.
—Oscar Wilde

He has the most who is most content with the least.
—Diogenes

Most people work just hard enough not to get fired and get paid just enough money not to quit.
—George Carlin

When the going gets weird, the weird turn pro.
—Hunter S. Thompson

The noble and the nobility are usually at odds with one another.
—Johann Gottfried Seume

We honor productivity to such an extent that the unproductive person or day seems a failure.
—Thomas Moore, *Meditations*

Try not to become a man of success, but rather try to become a man of value.
—Albert Einstein

The game is not about becoming somebody, it's about becoming nobody.
—Ram Dass

Men hate the individual whom they call avaricious only because nothing can be gained from him.
—Voltaire

There is nothing noble in being superior to your fellow man; true nobility is being superior to your former self.
—Ernest Hemingway

Why did pale-skinned Europeans become so powerful? All sagas of nations and battles, of explorations and inventions, and even of disease as a factor in conquest, conceal a nutritional key. Whites feed well because they conquered the world, but perhaps they conquered the world because they were well fed. Milk is five times more efficient that meat in converting grass into food energy for humans. The assurance against protein malnutrition conferred by the milk-drinking mutation traces back more than six thousand years to ancestors of speakers of Semitic, Indo-European and Uralic languages, and to the livestock of cow and plow.
—Nigel Calder, *Timescale*

When the power of love overcomes the love of power, the world will know peace.
—Jimi Hendrix

I'm sick of following my dreams. I'm just going to ask them where they're going and hook up with them later.
—Mitch Hedberg

Success, like happiness, cannot be pursued; it must ensue, and it only does so as the unintended side-effect of one's personal dedication to a cause greater than oneself or as the by-product of one's surrender to a person other than oneself.
—Viktor E. Frankl, *Man's Search for Meaning*

To laugh often and much; to win the respect of intelligent people and the affection of children…to leave the world a better place…to know even one life has breathed easier because you have lived. This is to have succeeded.
—Ralph Waldo Emerson

Power certainly corrupts, but that statement is humanly incomplete. Isn't it too abstract? What should certainly be added is the specific truth that having power destroys the sanity of the powerful. It allows their irrationalities to leave the sphere of dreams and come into the real world.
—Saul Bellow, *Mr. Sammler's Planet*

Too many people spend money they haven't earned, to buy things they don't want, to impress people they don't like.
—Will Rogers

Big things of the world can only be achieved by attending to their small beginnings.
—Lao Tzu, *The Tao Te Ching*, translated by John C. H. Wu

Thus instead of engaging is a "policy of small steps" toward a reasonable, reachable achievement, it is very useful to set oneself a goal that is admirably lofty. The advantages of this strategy should be immediately obvious to my readers…above all, if the goal is that high and distant, even the most stupid among us will understand that the road to that goal will be long and cumbersome, and that the travel will require extensive and time-consuming preparations. Therefore, who dares to blame us if we have not yet gotten started or if, once on our way, we get lost, march around in circles, or sit down for lengthy rests?
—Paul Watzlawik, *The Situation is Hopeless, But Not Serious*

Never counted among the dragons,
Never entered the lists of greats.
Always the wine sage,
Everywhere the verse seer.
A graduate of mists,
A drunken saint of river and lake.
Jokes and laughs were my official career;
Got stuck.
Wrote notes for forty years instead
On the mad and crazy wind and moon.
—Qiao Ji, *"Myself"*

There really wasn't much else to do. Make something, and die.
—Ian McEwan, *Amsterdam*

For the person for whom small things do not exist, the great is not great.
—José Ortega y Gasset, *Meditations on Quixote*

Strong Men Also Cry

A WORTHY FUCKIN' ADVERSARY

War and Politics

Though most first-time viewers regard *The Big Lebowski* as little more than a pastiche and parody of detective story conventions, it is arguably much more: namely, a grand epic of War and Peace.

Beginning as it does with George Bush Senior's moralizing declaration of war on Iraq in 1991 ("This aggression will not stand!") and ending with the mourning of a fallen soldier in a battle over nothing against those who believe in nothing, it's clear that—at least to some degree—the Coens wanted to look at the consequences of war though a kooky and kaleidoscopic lens. Given the timing of the film, released in 1998, it's hard not to perceive it as eerily prescient.

Much has been made about an incredible coincidence in *The Big Lebowski*. The movie starts out with the Dude in a supermarket, paying for a quart of half-and-half with a check. As he fills out the check, Bush Sr. is speaking through the TV at the checkout stand, announcing the start of the first Gulf War. The date on the check? *September 11, 1991.*

Exactly ten years to the day later, consequences of that very war would help bring down the curtain on twenty years of American peace and usher in what many have considered a political and military quagmire comparable to the one the U.S. waged in Vietnam.

This haunting declaration of hostilities is neatly bookended at the denouement of the film: Walter sits at the bowling alley ruminating on how much easier it will be to crush the desert-dwelling Iraqis than the canopy-jungled Viet Cong—a "worthy fucking adversary" in his estimation. It goes without saying that if he and the hawkish Bush dynasty are in search of a "worthy fucking adversary," they will find more than they bargained for ten years later: rotting remains, to some degree, of what Walter dismissively deems a "piece of cake."

Seconds later, in the bowling alley parking lot, Walter is compelled to defend himself and his friends against opponents far more hapless than even the Iraqis (German zealots—a distant and enfeebled echo of a former "worthy fucking adversary"). Yet even when offered an easy way out, he stands firm and dispatches them easily, fighting bravely for what he believes in.

The victory comes at an unforeseen and bitter price: At far too young an age, Dude and Walter's bowling teammate Donnie dies of a heart attack during the melee. Though the battle is won (saving them all the few dollars in their wallets), the balance sheet records a far greater loss, and a darkly absurd one at that. Coupled with imaginary sounds of "help chopperin' in," Donnie's death evokes those of soldiers who needlessly "died face down in the muck" alongside young Walter in Vietnam. It also (unbeknownst to the authors, of course) darkly portends the future political landscape of the United States.

As if echoing the frustrating ups and downs, strikes and gutters of an aggressive American foreign policy, Walter's knee-jerk decision to retaliate blows up in his face several times throughout the film. "You see what happens when you fuck a stranger in the ass?" Walter rebukes another of his many undeserving foes earlier in the movie, before executing yet another tragically misplaced and overwrought retribution. It is an ironic battle cry to be sure, as it is he, under various imaginary jurisdictions, who is doing all the strangerfucking. Of course, "what happens" each time is that his reluctant and naïve soldiers (Dude and Donnie) are obliged to suffer the fallout from his shambolic crusades.

The Coens may be smart fellers, but oracles as well? First of all, when *The Big Lebowski* was released in 1998 there was little indication that America would suffer any serious backlash from the first Gulf War, nor an unflinching, religiously sentimental support for Israel (lampooned in Walter's clinging to the adopted Orthodox Judaism of his ex-wife Cynthia).

Secondly, the idea of an angry America whipped into a neoconservative frenzy would have seemed fairly preposterous in 1998. For one thing, neo-conservatism was largely unfamiliar to the American public until George Bush Jr. helped give it wings, post-9/11. In fact, it's been successfully argued by David Haglund in *Slate* magazine that the first mass-culture neocon was not Bush II, but Walter Sobchak.

Finally, the notion that the hardened U.S. military juggernaut might prove tragically ineffective against the "camel fuckers" of the Middle East would have seemed just plain ridiculous at the end of the 20th century. And this is where the Saga of Sobchak really helps cut through the fog of war like headlights on a four-by-four: Our worthy fucking adversaries today are a categorically different menace than they were in the heydays of Black Pajamas (Vietnam) or National Socialism (Nazism). Say what you will.

Even if *The Big Lebowski* did prognosticate the New World Disorder more effectively than any number of bestselling political theorists, no one would be so foolhardy as to suggest that nations should look to the Dude for inspiration when drawing up foreign policy. Still, we might request of the military industrial complex "Will you just take it easy, man?" Here we can consult the *Tao Te Ching* for inspiration: Though primarily a book for personal growth, it regards nations as individuals writ large and contains a surprising amount of political and battlefield advice.

One of the recurring themes in The *Tao Te Ching* is that governments and military should exert their powers as little as possible over their constituents and adversaries, respectfully. The first is perhaps best illustrated by chapter 60's passage:

Manage a great nation
As you would cook a delicate fish.

In other words, don't fuck with a society too much or it will fall apart. Likewise, since war is an extension of politics (as the great military theorist Clausewitz maintained) the same approach should be applied to all things military: keep your spatula (or semi-automatic) holstered as much as possible. A surprising number of chapters of *The Tao Te Ching* explicitly advocate that rulers should avoid military conflict as much as possible, should discard imperial ambitions, and should treat war as a last resort only after all diplomatic ambitions have been exhausted. Modern hawks might pooh pooh these notions as naïve hippie pipe dreams, but they were also enshrined as well in Sun Tzu's *Art of War*, a treatise generally considered of major importance by generals and majors throughout history. Not exactly a lightweight.

To impose our ideals upon others by force is what Fascism is all about, and this is exactly antithetical to the view of the Tao, which at its core contends that "coercion is anathema to human flourishing" (according to Hall and Ames' commentary on the *Tao*). This helps explain why there are so many anti-fascist bon mots in *The Big Lebowski* ("fucking fascist!" "real reactionary," "those rich fucks!" "our basic freedoms," "the square community"). Yet, that both the Dude and Walter utter lines like these helps to show that our hierarchies of freedoms can ultimately be extremely varied. Should we be allowed to scream out loud in public family restaurants? Did the Vietnam War actually safeguard American liberty? Is employment a right or a requirement? Should we be allowed to hang out in nice, quiet beach communities even if we don't own property there? Are there rules to a ransom, or can one just wing it?

The divergence between the left-leaning Dude and the proto-Neoconservative Walter underscores the current schizophrenia evinced in the United States when it comes to freedom itself. Both the right wing and the left wing believe the other is composed of deluded idealists who would take away "our basic freedoms," only they differ upon what basis those basic freedoms might actually be based.

Given the current schism of isms in the USA, might anyone be interested in tying the room together by launching a Lebowskitarian Party? Could the world be ready for a true Dudeocracy?

Ahh, fuck it. It's probably a bad idea for us to face down the muck of politics here. Just as religion and politics are held at arm's length from each other by the American constitution, so might Dudeism refrain from outwardly interpreting government and its battlefield extrapolations. After all, what is politics other than an attempt to pave the road to the future? Policies and provisos are put in place to try to engineer a state better than the one we are in now. And none of us can ascertain what awaits us further on down the trail. Only delusional psychotics and well-paid proselytizers know what's coming next or how programs will play out. Furthermore, if there's one thing we've learned from history it's that very little is learned from history.

Consequently, the state Dudeism is primarily concerned with is the present one. We don't really care about anyone's personal political affiliation, national citizenship, or military philosophy. The world is far more confounding than it was in Lao Tzu's time. So anyone who finds all this too exhausting can join us in leaving the pundits, politicians, peaceniks and parochials to argue over which way is Westward. We'll just be sitting here watching their wheels go round and round. We sure as shit really love to watch them roll.

It's hard to believe how sick of war we used to be back then. We used to boast of how small our Army and Navy were, and how little influence generals and admirals had in Washington. We used to call armaments manufacturers "merchants of death."
—Kurt Vonnegut, *Bluebeard*

The purpose of war, Clausewitz said, was to serve a political end; the nature of war, he succeeded in arguing, was to serve only itself. By conclusion, his logic therefore ran, those who make war an end in itself are likely to be more successful than those who seek to moderate its character for political purposes. The peace of the most peaceful century in European history was held ransom to this subversive idea, which bubbled and seethed like the flux of an active volcano beneath the surface of progress and prosperity.
—John Keegan, *A History Of Warfare*

It is lamentable, that to be a good patriot one must become the enemy of the rest of mankind.
—Voltaire

Ohhh. Great warrior. Wars not make one great.
—Master Yoda, *The Empire Strikes Back* (1980). Screenplay by Leigh Brackett

Nationalism is an infantile disease. It is the measles of mankind.
—Albert Einstein

Patriotism is the willingness to kill and be killed for trivial reasons.
—Bertrand Russell

We spend so much money on the military, yet we're slashing education budgets throughout the country. No wonder we've got smart bombs and stupid fucking children.
—Jon Stewart

"You know what I say to people when I hear they're writing anti-war books? Why don't you write an anti-*glacier* book instead?"
    What he meant, of course, was that there would always be wars, and that they were as easy to stop as glaciers. I believe that too.
—Kurt Vonnegut, *Slaughterhouse Five*

A nation is a society united by a delusion about its ancestry and by common hatred of its neighbors.
—William Inge

War, organized war, is not a human instinct. It is a highly planned and cooperative form of theft.
—Jacob Bronowski, *The Ascent Of Man*

Many a man will have the courage to die gallantly, but will not have the courage to say, or even to think, that the cause for which he is asked to die is an unworthy one.
—Bertrand Russell

There ain't no revolution, only evolution. But every time I'm in Georgia I eat a peach for peace.
—Duane Allman

Terms like "the free world" and "the national interest" and so on are mere terms of propaganda. One shouldn't take them seriously for a moment. They are designed, often very consciously, in order to try to block thought and understanding.
—Noam Chomsky, *Chronicles of Dissent*

The largest party in America, by the way, is neither the Democrats nor the Republicans. It's the party of non-voters.
—Robert Reich

You know, I think the main purpose of the Army, Navy, and Marine Corps is to get poor Americans into clean, pressed, unpatched clothes, so rich Americans can stand to look at them.
—Kurt Vonnegut, *God Bless You Mr. Rosewater*

Political language—and with variations this is true of all political parties, from Conservatives to Anarchists—is designed to make lies sound truthful and murder respectable, and to give an appearance of solidity to pure wind.
—George Orwell, *Politics and the English Language*

Government is so tedious that sometimes you wonder if the government isn't being boring on purpose. Maybe they're trying to put us to sleep so we won't notice what they're doing.
—P.J. O'Rourke, *Parliament of Whores*

The whole aim of practical politics is to keep the populace alarmed (and hence clamorous to be led to safety) by menacing it with an endless series of hobgoblins, all of them imaginary.
—H.L. Mencken

Patriots always talk of dying for their country and never of killing for their country.
—Bertrand Russell

The next time they give you all that civic bullshit about voting, keep in mind that Hitler was elected in a full, free democratic election.
—George Carlin

Politics, as a practice, whatever its professions, has always been the systematic organization of hatreds.
—Henry Adams

Territoriality—the drive to gain, maintain, and defend the exclusive right to a piece of property—is an animal instinct approximately as ancient as sex.
—Robert Ardrey, *African Genesis*

War is the health of the State. It automatically sets in motion throughout society those forces for uniformity, for passionate cooperation with the Government in coercing into obedience the minority groups and individuals which lack the larger herd sense.
—Randolph Bourne

I can picture in my mind a world without war, a world without hate. And I can picture us attacking that world, because they'd never expect it.
—Jack Handey, *Deep Thoughts*

Abstract words such as glory, honor, courage, or hallow were obscene beside the concrete names of villages, the numbers of roads, the names of rivers, the numbers of regiments and dates.
—Ernest Hemingway, *A Farewell to Arms*

I am not only a pacifist but a militant pacifist. I am willing to fight for peace. Nothing will end war unless the people themselves refuse to go to war.
—Albert Einstein

Nationalism has usurped the place of Religion as the most important super-individual interest of individuals. [It] has indeed in some sense become a religion.
—Julian Huxley, *Essays Of A Biologist*

The Pact of Paris, [1928] properly known as the General Treaty for the Renunciation of War, explicitly committed the signatories to resolve all disputes in the future "by pacific means." Thereafter, all warmaking was technically illegal.
—John Keegan, *A History Of Warfare*

A government which robs Peter to pay Paul can always depend on the support of Paul.
—George Bernard Shaw

Love, friendship and respect do not unite people as much as a common hatred for something.
—Anton Chekov

Eternal vigilance is the price of freedom. Insanity is the price of eternal vigilance.
—Mark Vonnegut, *Eden Express*

Dudemerica

THE FUCKIN' EAGLES, MAN

The United States of America

There once was a time when the rest of the world was in love with the United States. In the middle to late part of the 20th century, the U.S. stood as a symbol of freedom and honor and hot chicks and hot rods and hot dogs and other things that were considered hot. Today, not so much. Generally, the rest of the world perceives America as a bit arrogant if not downright cruel. Of course, part of the reason for this is simply because it's become the richest, most powerful nation on the planet by far. What can one expect? An alpha dog is always seen as domineering by definition.

Of course, there are other, legitimate, reasons that the world is ambivalent about America, such as a manipulative foreign policy, its consumption of the majority of the world's resources, and the fact that U.S. citizens and politicians are so proud of stating that theirs is the best and freest country in the world, despite knowing so little about the other 192, several of which are arguably superior in some areas and freer as well. On the other hand, people in the other 192 seem to know everything about America, often more than the average American citizen.

In fact, that average American citizen would be amazed just how intimately knowledgeable the entire world is with the tiniest fashion trend, nervous whim or current terror of the American populace. How could they possibly know so much about a land and a people so far away?

It's not just that they're reading Cosmopolitan in Khmer or The New York Times in Nahuatl. More broadly, they're getting all this inside information from America's vast output of movies. For the last few decades, cheap rip offs of American films and increasingly, TV shows, have saturated the planet as if part of an alien invasion. The shiny metallic discs they often travel on even look a bit like 1960s-style UFOs.

Unfortunately for Yankee public relations, many of even the most impoverished of Earth's citizens spend much of their free time watching muscular American military commandoes gun down legions of dark-skinned lunatics, whiny American adolescents complain about how they're not getting laid enough, and wealthy middle-aged

American housewives quest for something meaningful in their lives beyond home decorating and affairs with the gardener.

It's a shame that so few of the world's citizens have seen rare and unusual American films like *The Big Lebowski*. It would be helpful if they understood that Americans are not as confident about everything as they seem and that they harbor doubts and worries and misgivings about the high-profile *isms* of their civilization (capitalism, militarism, idealism). Mainstream Hollywood movies don't let on that the U.S. is a much more subtle and deeply textured nation than our movies and political policies would indicate.

This book has postulated aplenty about all the different things *The Big Lebowski* might be all about. Here's one more: it's all about America. That is not just to say it's a film that takes place in the United States, nor that it shines a spotlight upon aspects of the country. One might earnestly argue that the entire subject of the film is the country itself, or at least, the *idea* of America.

This would explain a lot: why we have a cowboy-as-narrator, the president of the country speaking the first line of the film, and more Yankee cultural nostalgia than you'd find at an outdoor swap meet (The Wild West, Vietnam, the 'Sixties, German adversaries, Film Noir detectives and their femmes fatales, burgers, bowling, car culture, country music, porn). It's like a giant "You Are Here" map for the American soul, annotated with subtle but salient points of interest. Some have noticed, for instance, that the knit Pendleton sweater the Dude wears upon meeting the cowboy narrator for the first time bears a traditional Native American weaving pattern[7]. Dances with Wool?

Furthermore, the defining "nation of immigrants" hallmark is hammered home via a cast of conspicuously non-Anglo descent: There's a bunch of Poles, a few Latinos, a Greek, two Italians, a "Chinaman," a Jew (by conversion), several Germans, a farm girl of Swedish extraction, an Iranian doctor, and an Irishman to boot. In fact, outside of maybe Arthur Digby Sellers and his son Larry—both of whom are tellingly mute—there are virtually no White Anglo-Saxon Protestants in the entire film. Oh, except for Knox Harrington, who is evidently a native Liverpudlian. With a cleft asshole. And anyway, he's probably Anglican.

The Big Lebowski is thus an immigrant epic, about people freed from convention, trying to forge their own identity, and having somewhat of an awkward time of it. Everyone in the movie is essentially putting on an act, trying to redefine themselves, to break away from whatever their true history may actually be. Their ideas consequently clash, sometimes violently. But in the end, truth peers out from behind the masks, if only briefly.

The Declaration of Dudependence, ultimately, might then be this: As a mash up of peoples, we might understandably be a bit of a mess; but on the other hand, it ain't

---

[7] Actually, the Cowichan Indians who designed the pattern are from an area which is now Canada. But that's still in the Americas. Let's not split hairs, eh?

easy blazing new trails, trying to get along, trying to take it easy with all the stupefyin' changes going on, and still trying to continue pushing those wagons westward, even if we're at the limit of the land and not sure where to go from here.

The human face of a nation too often known by its idealistic and arrogant mask may be just the thing the world needs to see revealed. In a country famous for mighty individualism, the Dude stands out precisely because he is a bit the opposite: unsteady and skeptical but open to new ideas and eager to make new friends.

What's more, the fact that his character is so beloved by such a broad swath of America's citizenry suggests that we too might be happy to see our nation engage in a lot less kicking ass, and a lot more kicking back.

I wasn't like my parents. I didn't have any supposedly sacred piece of land or shoals or friends or relatives to leave behind. Nowhere has the number zero been more of philosophical value than in the United States.

"Here goes nothing," says the American as he goes off the high diving board.
—Kurt Vonnegut, *Bluebeard*

There are people all over the world who are willing to exploit others. You can't just point the finger at America.
—Arlo Guthrie

Myths and legends die hard in America. We love them for the extra dimension they provide, the illusion of near-infinite possibility to erase the narrow confines of most men's reality. Weird heroes and mold-breaking champions exist as living proof to those who need it that the tyranny of "the rat race" is not yet final.
—Hunter S. Thompson, *The Great Shark Hunt: Strange Tales from a Strange Time*

I like America, just as everybody else does. I love America, I gotta say that. But America will be judged.
—Bob Dylan

What is the basis for our union as a people? It cannot be the English language, because too many Americans do not speak the language or speak it badly. It cannot be the Constitution because too many Americans do not know what it says and if they did, would repudiate it. I submit that, lacking the usual grounds on which people congregate as a nation, we habitually fall back on the most primitive yet most enduring basis for group cohesion, namely, scapegoating.
—Thomas Szasz, *Our Right to Drugs*

It wouldn't be far-fetched to suggest that in *Lebowski* bowling seems to stand for the American dream of real friendship between people from different backgrounds and ethnicities, even if the point is disguised by absurdity. The bowling alley is a place where people can be themselves—among the film's most beautiful sequences is the one in which we simply watch folks bowl.
—J.M. Tyree & Ben Walters, *BFI Film Classics: The Big Lebowski*

America is the interplay of three hundred million Rube Goldberg contraptions invented only yesterday.
—Kurt Vonnegut, *Timequake*

In Chinese folklore, worth is disguised as a beggar; power always lies hidden. Whereas on our television, the best is all out in front.
—Camille Paglia, *Sex, Art and American Culture*

Today few could speak the language of the Enlightenment: "We hold these truths to be self-evident…" For today's scholars these words hide as much as they state. No truths are self-evident; they are constructed and invented. They emerge at specific times and places; these are "truths" of eighteenth-century Europe and America. And who is the "We?" A bunch of white patricians?
—Russell Jacoby, *The End of Utopia*

Conventional wisdom has it that Los Angeles' sprawl is a consequence of its extensive post-war freeway system. In fact, it was because the city was sprawling already that freeways were thought a practical way of connecting far-flung parts. It sprawled because it had the finest public transportation network in America, if not the world, with over a thousand miles of rail and trolley lines…

   Between 1922 and 1932…a company called National City Lines—a cartel made up of General Motors and a collection of oil and rubber interests—began buying up trolley lines and converting them to bus routes. By 1950 it had closed down the streetcar systems of more than a hundred cities.
—Bill Bryson, *Made in America*

As a metaphor, the California of pulp [fiction] brought the intellectual processes of the 19th century to a bad end. The promise of reinvention, so vital to the American Renaissance, unraveled into a hive of false identity, where no one was what he or she seemed.
—John Leland, *Hip: The History*

The person who insists upon being a hundred percent American has by that very emphasis become something less than half a man.
—Lewis Mumford, *The Story of Utopias*

Middle-Eastern scholars like Bernard Lewis argue that the Islamic world, once a leader in arts and technology, lost its edge when it repressed contradictory ideas, particularly those of women. It shut itself off from the outside. The United States, by contrast, thrived because of the cacophony of ideas—not a melting pot but an unmelted melee. Its noise is the sound of growth.
—John Leland, *Hip: The History*

America is not only big and rich, it is mysterious; and its capacity for the humorous or ironical concealment of its interests matches that of the legendary inscrutable Chinese.
—David Riesman, *The Lonely Crowd*

I sometimes think we ought to bring a bill before Congress changing our national symbol from the eagle to the buffalo, because we are more like the buffalo than the eagle. The eagle is a powerful bird. It flies alone. It rises up into the sky with authority. It is master of all it surveys. The eagle is an individualist and was selected from among the rest of the birds to be our symbol. But the buffalo was never alone. It always ran in a herd with other buffaloes. And, friends, I call your attention that the buffaloes are gone from the open range, but the eagles are still soaring.
—Norman Vincent Peale

In the United States there is more space where nobody is than where anybody is. That is what makes America what it is.
—Gertrude Stein, *The Geographical History of America*

The three great American vices seem to be efficiency, punctuality, and the desire for achievement and success. They are the things that make the Americans so unhappy and so nervous.
—Lin Yutang, *The Importance of Living*

America is so vast that almost everything said about it is likely to be true, and the opposite is probably equally true.
—James T. Farrell

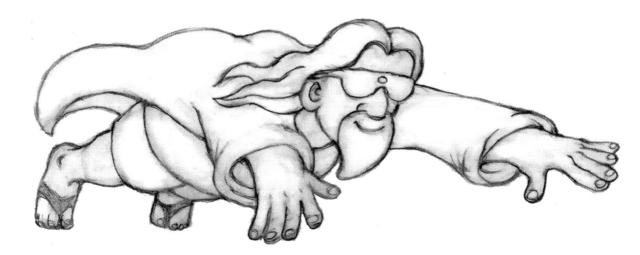

Dudeman

WHAT'S A HEE-RO?

Heroism

There was a time, long ago, when heroes and their stories were relatively rare. Cavemen, for instance, were continually forced to sit around the campfire and tell the same tale of good old Doog who selflessly threw himself in front of a charging lion to save his special lady Mog, while glossing over the fact that Mog actually pushed him. Such is the need for heroes—even when there are none around, we're obliged to dream them up. Otherwise, we'd have to admit how defenseless we are against all those lions out there.

Our fantasy world has enlarged immensely since those caveman days. Now that books and movies and television have taken the place of the campfire, we no longer have to repeat the same tired tales. In fact there are so many to choose from that the concept of "hero" has fairly broadened in value. Today everybody's a revolutionary. Guerrillas in our midst include: politicians standing up for the interest (and votes) of the downtrodden; sports stars elevating the poor and simultaneously their public image; erstwhile pushers of crack, now purveyors of Christ; debauched rock stars demanding moral action at "aid" festivals; and Hollywood actors skillfully acting concerned about world affairs.

There's a type of sandwich popular in the US called a "hero"—it's basically a big baguette full of baloney and cheese. Never has a dish been more perfectly named. Art mirrors reality, and in some cases, arteriosclerosis.

Forgive us while we drive the metaphor into the ground: the Dude makes such a refreshing alternative to the heroic ham-fist because his process is totally unprocessed. Just as every culture has its version of the sandwich (burrito, crepe, *bao*, *samosa*, etc.), the Dudeist sandwich is the In-N-Out Burger; it is indulgent and fortifying while at the same time healthy, unpretentious and affordable.

Setting the stage, the opening narration of *The Big Lebowski* ironically casts that original specter of old-fashioned Yankee do-goodism in the person of the anonymous, omniscient cowboy. Introducing "the Dude" in his opening monologue, the Stranger's grizzled voiceover intones: "Sometimes there's a man—I won't say a hero, 'cause what's a hero?—but sometimes there's a man...well, he's the man for his time and place. He fits right in there."

Importantly, the narrator explains that the story takes place in the early 90s, during the time of "our conflict with Sad'm and the Eye-rackies." That is, when that big plains sheriff (the US military) came off its long cold-war sabbatical and, guns a-blazing, resumed kicking outlaw ass. It was just like the good old days, when God was on our side and the bad guys wore black pajamas. Yippie-ki-yay, camelfucker.

But, make no mistake, the Dude is indeed a hero, though not in the timeworn cartoonish sense of the word. If a hero is someone who truly goes against the grain and stands up for what he knows to be right, then the Dude, by standing up (or sitting down rather) for the virtues of "taking it easy" in the face of smug entreaties to "Just Do It," and to "draw a line in the sand," should be by all definitions a hero of the first rank. The narrator only demurs because he knows the word no longer means what it once did.

It seems that the concept of the "hero" became diluted over the years largely due to the work of a 20th century scholar named Joseph Campbell. In searching for the universal concept of meaning, this "master of myth" dissected all the world's stories and came up with a framework that described, at length, what it meant to be a hero, and what was his function in society.

It's arguable that Campbell has had more influence on the way we think about the human drama today than Shakespeare ever did. That's because at some point in those same early 90s, every screenwriter in Hollywood was presented a brief outline of Campbell's ideas called "The Hero's Journey" and instructed to follow it to the letter. Of course they all obeyed. After all, it was the secret code to the unconscious: the genome of dramatic conflict, the treasure map to box-office mammon. It was as if Moses had come down off the mountain with a slew of cinematic commandments handed down directly from God. Or possibly Steven Spielberg.

The consequences were cinemato-strophic: The subsequent decade or two were the most ridiculous in film history, with scripts written as if by robots, star salaries approaching the budgets of entire nations, and formula flicks like *Braveheart* and *Titanic* taking home the lion's share of the Academy Awards. The Jesus wept.

Yet despite what many religions, movies, and other fictions might imply, the human condition cannot be reduced to a mimeographed list of playwright's precepts. This is precisely why most films today seem so industrially shaped, packaged and full of crap: The cinematic hero has in fact become identical to its lunch-line namesake: boxy, reheated junk food. What's grist for the movie mill are Big Macs for the mind.

Though *The Big Lebowski* has since developed into a massive cult hit, it failed dismally upon its initial release, no doubt due in part to the fact that the movie blatantly disregarded the orthodox scripture of Hollywood. Among other things, it wholeheartedly stomped on the sacred tenets of screenwriting, including: a) confirm the audience's prejudices, b) have the protagonist accomplish something—*anything*,

c) never resort to a narrator, and most importantly of all—d) never indulge in dialogue for its own sake.

What is most ironic is that, in religiously embracing Campbell's hero myth, Hollywood, its heroes, and its audience became intolerant, rigidly one-dimensional and ossified. Yet these were the very traits Campbell's archetypal heroes were meant to rail against in the first place.

The Dudeist hero is a redeemer not only of the disenfranchised, but of the very franchise of heroism itself. He is the one who marches, or slouches, to the beat of his own drummer, even if that drummer is offbeat compared to everyone else in the orchestra. The square community may not give a shit about him, but that's just their market-researched and focus-grouped opinion.

Fortunately, not everyone's thinking about this has become very uptight—witness the resurgence of creative programming on alternative broadcast streams which don't live and die by massive box office weekend openings. We happen to know that there are many Little Big Lebowskis on the way. And so finally we may no longer have to sit through Doog's same old timeworn campfire yarn. Hopefully our received notions of heroism will also evolve accordingly.

We do so much, we run so quickly, the situation is difficult and many people say, "Don't just sit there, do something." But doing more things may make the situation worse. So you should say, "Don't just do something, sit there."
—Thich Nhat Hanh, *Being Peace*

When it is not necessary to make a decision, it is necessary not to make a decision.
—Lord Falkland

There is no greatness without goodness.
—Ernest Wood, *Concentration*

The wonderful thing for us, she went on, "is that Jesus was a man, no more able to do miracles and no more likely to have them done for him than the rest of us. Just a man—and yet he could do what he did, he could be what he was. That's the wonder."
—Aldous Huxley, *Eyeless in Gaza*

He who has not the spirit of this age, has all the misery of it.
—Voltaire

The mighty and great will be laid low;
The humble and weak will be exalted.
—Lao Tzu, *The Tao Te Ching*, translated by John C. H. Wu

And whosoever shall exalt himself shall be humbled: and he that shall humble himself shall be exalted.
—Jesus Christ, *Matthew 23:12*

The greatest strength is gentleness.
—*Iroquois Indian Proverb*

If there is a human moral to be drawn, it is that we must *teach* our children altruism, for we cannot expect it to be part of their biological nature.
—Richard Dawkins, *The Selfish Gene*

The highest good is like water,
Water gives life to the ten thousand things and does not strive.
It flows in places men reject and so is like the Tao.
—Lao Tzu, *The Tao Te Ching*, translated by Gia-Fu Feng and Jane English

Heroing is one of the shortest-lived professions there is.
—Will Rogers

It is best to be a coward for a minute than dead for the rest of your life.
—*Irish proverb*

A prophet is not without honor, except in his own country, among his own kin, and in his own house.
—Jesus Christ, *Mark 6:4*

When a true genius appears in the world you may know him by this sign; that the dunces are all in confederacy against him.
—Jonathan Swift

The private eye was his own invention, usually an independent operator, unmarried, childless, and motherless. He cowed neither to women nor to work. He did not suffer an employer; in many stories he gained the upper hand by walking away from a check. Similarly, he cut a sexual swath but did not have any attachments or obligations…
    The pulp hero, the first hip icon that did not rely on the East Coast bohemia or intelligentsia, drew on the character of the western outlaw, but without the tragic fatalism. The detectives were not criminals, but not exactly law-abiding. They were a different mix of the civilized and the primitive, able to dip into either when needed.
—John Leland, *Hip: The History*

What lies behind us and what lies before us are small matters compared to what lies within us.
—Ralph Waldo Emerson

I knew that what I was seeking to discover was a thing I'd always known. That all courage was a form of constancy. That it was always himself that the coward abandoned first. After this all other betrayals came easily.
—Cormac McCarthy, *All the Pretty Horses*

There is one fault that I must find
With the twentieth century,
And I'll put it in a couple of words:
Too adventury.
What I'd like would be some nice dull monotony
If anyone's gotony.
—Ogden Nash, *"Put Back Those Whiskers, I Know You"*

The clown is He Who Gets Slapped—and is none the worse for his slapping. He is resilient with a vitality lacking in the tragic hero.
—Wylie Sypher, *Our New Sense of the Comic*

Heroism is simply a matter of facing the truth.
—Kwai Chang Caine, *Kung Fu: The Legend Continues*

Show me a hero and I will show you a tragedy.
—F. Scott Fitzgerald

Excused from the tiring, vain, arbitrary business of being a man, [the Dude] can concentrate instead on being human.
—J.M. Tyree & Ben Walters, *BFI Film Classics: The Big Lebowski*

He had said, "I am a man," and that meant certain things to Juana. It meant that he was half insane and half god. It meant that Kino would drive his strength against a mountain and plunge his strength against the sea. Juana, in her woman's soul knew the mountain would stand while the man broke himself; that the sea would surge while the man drowned in it. And yet it was this thing that made him a man, half-insane and half god.
—John Steinbeck, *The Pearl*

The wild boar runs from the tiger, knowing that each be well-armed by nature with deadly strength, may kill the other. Running, he saves his own life and that of the tiger. This is not cowardice. It is the love of life.
—Master Kan, *Kung Fu (1972)*, Season 1, Episode 9. Script by Robert Lewin

[The History of Increasing Humiliation] would be a book accounting for the decline in status of literary protagonists. First gods, then demigods, then kings, then great warriors, great lovers, then burghers and merchants and vicars and doctors and lawyers. Then social realism: you. Then irony: me. Then maniacs and murderers, tramps, mobs, rabble, flotsam, vermin...the history of astronomy is the history of increasing humiliation. First the geocentric universe, then the heliocentric universe. Then the eccentric universe—the one we're living in. Every century we get smaller...Big book. Small world. Big Universe.
—Martin Amis, *The Information*

The human organism, which seemed an independent unit, capable of acting by itself, is placed in its physical environment like a figure in a tapestry. It is no longer the organism that moves but the environment that is moving through it...Darwin sweeps heroes off the face of the earth.
—Joseph Cambell, *Creative Mythology*

A hero is someone who understands the responsibility that comes with his freedom.
—Bob Dylan

My belt holds my pants up, but the belt loops hold my belt up. So which one's the real hero?
—Mitch Hedberg

When you are content to be simply yourself and don't compare or compete, everybody will respect you.
—Lao Tzu, *The Tao Te Ching,* translated by Stephen Mitchell

Society everywhere is in conspiracy against the manhood of every one of its members. Society is a joint-stock company, in which the members agree, for the better securing of his bread to each shareholder, to surrender the liberty and culture of the eater. The virtue in most request is conformity. Self-reliance is its aversion. It loves not realities and creators, but names and customs.

Whoso would be a man, must be a nonconformist. He who would gather immortal palms must not be hindered by the name of goodness, but must explore if it be goodness. Nothing is at last sacred but the integrity of your own mind.
—Ralph Waldo Emerson

[Moses] is a man who does not think highly of himself, who never relies on his own talents, only on God's word. He was, as Exodus says of him, "the humblest man on earth," an extraordinary description in a world of boastful heroes. In his humility he has been hollowed out like a reed, so there is nothing in him—no pride or quirk of personality—to distort God's message. He can serve, therefore as an authentic medium, a true channel.
—Thomas Cahill, *The Gifts of the Jews*

Heroes ain't born; they're cornered.
—Redd Foxx

Ortega takes care to warn us that we are all heroes in some measure, that heroism is not ascribed to certain specific contents of life, that it lies dormant everywhere as a possibility, that the will is the tragic theme. In other words, that heroism and tragedy belong essentially to man, as forms of being in which life rids itself of its merely biological condition and exhibits its true nature. Don Quixote is the paradigm of that nature...His is a *frontier nature*, and it is manifested in the very condition of man.
—Julián Marías, from the introduction to *Meditations on Quixote*, by José Ortega y Gasset

If we refuse to have our actions determined by heredity or environment, it is because we seek to base the origin of our actions on ourselves and only ourselves. The hero's will is not that of his ancestors nor of his society, but his own. The will to be oneself is heroism.
—José Ortega y Gasset, *Meditations on Quixote*

The universe *is* inscrutable, unfathomable, malicious, *so*—like the white whale and his element. Art in the broad sense of all humanizing effort is man's answer to this condition…Not tame and gentle bliss, but disaster, heroically encountered, is man's true happy ending.
—Lewis Mumford, *Herman Melville*

Its first manufacturer, the German pharmaceutical company Friedrich Bayer, christened their product Heroin to suggest the German adjective *heroisch*, or heroic.
—John Leland, *Hip: The History*

Ph. Dude

A WISER FELLER THAN MYSELF ONCE SAID

Knowledge and Education

There is one scene in *The Big Lebowski* which, like a hologram, might be said to contain the rest of the movie—it is the scene where the Dude is introduced to his namesake's "hall of achievement." Like the Time "Man of the Year" mirror which marks the scene's end, it reflects everything which surrounds it.

The amazing thing about the script of *The Big Lebowski* is how unexpectedly exacting it is. Every mumble, waffle and stutter in the film was scripted that way. It may be hard to believe, but the Dude's tortured "blathering" in the limousine scene is written exactly as Jeff Bridges delivers it, down to every last articulately inarticulate "uh."

When the Big Lebowski's assistant Brandt (played by Phillip Seymour Hoffman) gives the Dude a tour of his boss' wall of plaques and achievements, he introduces his "Urban Achievers" charity by explaining that they are inner-city kids who "lack the necessary means for a, necessary means for a higher education…"

That is, he awkwardly repeats the words "necessary means" for no apparent reason. Aside from the fact that it's funny to see him flounder, why does otherwise eloquent Brandt stutter here, and only here? Even his boss' wife offers the Dude a thousand-dollar blowjob, Brandt manages to produce a parry as skilful as one might expect under the circumstances.

As it turns out, the "necessary means" (money) is exactly what the Big Lebowski is planning to embezzle from the charity. Fawning sycophant that he is, we can assume that Brandt knows everything about his shenanigans, and that a tiny hiccup of worry gets stuck in his tell-tale throat. Far out.

Yet even more important even than foreshadowing the solution to the central mystery of the movie, this pivotal early scene reveals the personas of not just the millionaire Lebowski, but the Dude Lebowski as well. Though we may not see it right away, in hindsight it speaks even more to the uncommon accomplishments of the Dude than it does to those of the Big Lebowski himself.

In this "anteroom of achievement" the Dude has entered an alternate universe in which he gets to envision how his own life might have turned out had he not spent so much time in college smoking Thai stick, bowling and occupying R.O.T.C. buildings. Had he applied himself, he too might have also gone off to fight a war in Asia, struggled upwardly mobile, emerged a great "philanthropist," and married a sexy young trophy wife. Just like his namesake.

When Brandt tells him about the Urban Achievers charity, middle-aged Dude semi-jokingly asks him if they've got room for one more. Evidently he too lacks the "necessary means." The sequence terminates with the hilarious slap in the face: Dude staring into his own puzzled reflection on a mirrored mock-up of Time Magazine which bears the headline: "Are you a Lebowski Achiever?" Somehow, he ended up on the wrong side of the looking glass.

In today's "information economy" more so than ever before, educational degrees can make an enormous difference to social standing. The widening gap between rich and poor in the USA and many other countries is due largely to the earning difference between the highly-educated and the semi-educated or uneducated workforce. Of course, the Big Lebowski's fortune didn't have anything to do with his education—he merely married into money—but we don't know that yet.

Despite the Dude's lack of achievement, he's clearly wiser than the average fellow and boasts a home full of books both erudite and eccentric (you'll need the high definition version of the film to discover what they are). Rather than making up a strict regimen, his knowledge and education have accumulated incidentally as a side effect of recreation—not with any goal in mind, but merely for its own sake. Thirteen years of mandatory schooling, not to mention college, end up being such a drag for most people that most of them forget that learning can be great fun; a dilettante's approach to education can be a pleasant and lifelong pursuit even if you never went to college, or didn't actually learn anything while you were there.

For most people, a college education represents merely a piece of paper, or a few lines on a resume. Even the Dude admits he doesn't really remember anything from his studies. But then, who does? The comedian Father Guido Sarducci (Don Novello) had a great old bit in the 70s called the "Five Minute University" where you learn in five minutes all the things you're actually going to remember after four years of college. Economics 101, for instance, consists of memorizing the phrase "supply and demand." That's it.

What, then, is the point of spending four years and tens of thousands of dollars? The point is that by earning a degree you've proven that you can perform sustained mental chores and finish tasks on time. It's not education you get from college, surely, but discipline, organizational skills, and most importantly for the adolescent, easy access to sex, drugs and booze.

All this leads one to believe that higher education might well be one of the biggest scams of our era. And since college fees in America have been rising far faster than inflation should dictate, it has emerged as an increasingly rapacious rip-off.

A far better idea: for a tiny fraction of four years' tuition, an adolescent could hire a private tutor for a few months to teach the necessary time-management skills and still have enough left over to properly fund college-style social events full of liquor, dope and dry-humping.

The only caveat to this is that maybe—just maybe—it was in college that the Dude learned an important lesson, one which would inspire his subsequent lifestyle, setting him on his humble traipse towards the transcendent. Maybe he saw that the whole thing was a scam and that the rat race of career would be even more pointless and exploitative than the brat race of university. Perhaps what the Dude learned in college was not to waste his life following the same bullshit agenda that would turn the Big Lebowski into an emasculated, compromised old hypocrite. Or perhaps he just discovered that so-called "higher education" was not so high after all, and no real match for reading a lot and hanging out at coffeehouses like the *fin de siècle* Dudes from whom he adopted his moniker.

The real-life inspiration for the Dude was a real person, a film producer by the name of Jeff Dowd. Dowd did in fact earn notoriety in his university years for actually being part of the Seattle Seven, a group which organized protests against the U.S. involvement in the Vietnam War, an enterprise we now know to be fraudulently conceived and inhumanely executed.

Whatever his grades were when he graduated, Mr. Dowd surely earned a *magna cum laude* in real life. We should all aspire to the same honorific. Self-knowledge should be considered the most necessary mean of all.

Being a good conversationalist is really what a liberal arts education is all about.
—Mark Vonnegut, *The Eden Express*

We are here and it is now. Further than that all human knowledge is moonshine.
—H. L. Mencken

We are faced with the paradoxical fact that education has become one of the chief obstacles to intelligence and freedom of thought.
—Bertrand Russell

A Greek olive-oil merchant living in Miletus 2600 years ago suggested that the world was made of water; with that guess, not a bad one, he launched the enterprises of physics and philosophy, and put the species to its biggest gamble: the bet that organized knowledge would do more good than harm.
—Nigel Calder, *Timescale*

All that could be learned from history was that history itself was absolutely nonsensical, so study something else, like music.
—Kurt Vonnegut, *Timequake*

The illiterate of the 21st century will not be those who cannot read and write, but those who cannot learn, unlearn, and relearn.
 —Anonymous (though often erroneously attributed to Alvin Toffler)

Why do you try to "enlarge" your mind? Subtilize it.
—Herman Melville, *Moby Dick*

College: A fountain of knowledge where all go to drink.
—Henny Youngman

How can I know what I think before I see what I say?
—E.M. Forster

By definition, both force and wealth are the property of the strong and the rich. It is the truly revolutionary characteristic of knowledge that it can be grasped by the weak and the poor as well. Knowledge is the most democratic source of power.
—Alvin and Heidi Toffler, *War and Anti-War*

Education is an admirable thing, but it is well to remember from time to time that nothing that is worth knowing can be taught.
—Oscar Wilde

If you want to get laid, go to college. If you want an education, go to the library.
—Frank Zappa

The only thing that interferes with my learning is my education.
—Albert Einstein

We don't know a millionth of a percent about anything.
—Thomas Alva Edison

You can get help from teachers, but you are going to have to learn a lot by yourself, sitting alone in a room.
—Theodor Geisel (Dr. Seuss)

Education consists mainly in what we have unlearned.
—Mark Twain

Man should not always find himself confined to the higher values discovered up to the present: science and justice, art and religion. In due time Pleasure will find its Newton and Ambition its Kant.
—José Ortega y Gasset, *Meditations on Quixote*

Much education today is monumentally ineffective. All too often we are giving young people cut flowers when we should be teaching them to grow their own plants.
—John W. Gardner

Have the courage to be ignorant of a great number of things, in order to avoid the calamity of being ignorant of everything.
—Sydney Smith

An ignorant person is one who doesn't know what you have just found out.
—Will Rogers

Beware of someone who wants to teach you something.
—George Gurdjieff

A library is an arsenal of liberty.
—Anonymous

The quality of strength lined with tenderness is an unbeatable combination, as are intelligence and necessity when unblunted by formal education.
—Maya Angelou, *"I Know Why the Caged Bird Sings"*

What we become depends on what we read after all of the professors have finished with us. The greatest university of all is a collection of books.
—Thomas Carlyle

It is not enough to have a good mind; the main thing is to use it well.
—Rene Descartes

It is a miracle that curiosity survives formal education.
—Albert Einstein

An education isn't how much you have committed to memory, or even how much you know. It's being able to differentiate between what you know and what you don't.
—Anatole France

Education is a progressive discovery of our own ignorance.
—Will Durant

I wonder whether, perhaps without realizing it, we seek out the books we need to read. Or whether books themselves, which are intelligent entities, detect their readers and catch their eye. In the end, every book is the I Ching. You pick it up, open it, and there it is, there you are.
—Andrés Neuman

Green with Rust Coloration

NEW SHIT HAS COME TO LIGHT

Progress

It's easy to forget that "progress" is a relatively new invention in the history of human culture. Until quite recently, humans lived in rather stable conditions and "progress" was the same for everyone: growing up, getting married, having kids and not incurring the wrath of unseen forces like God, ghosts and gingivitis. Ninety-nine percent of the population could not aspire to anything "better" because there was no way to improve one's lot other than supplication to the gods—a technique which worked about as well back then as it does today.

Way back in ancient Greece and Rome there was a brief moment when the idea of socio-cultural progress almost did take root. However, this peak of civilization was eventually quashed by greed (fucking fascists), degeneration (standards had fallen in adult entertainment), new superstitions (The Big LePopeski), and Barbarian invasions (fucking Germans—nothing changes).

The rebirth of progress is commonly held to have taken place around the scientific revolution of the 1600s. That was when people discovered that by using the scientific method the world could be made sense of rationally, rather than via religious intermediaries like the church or shamanistic oracles. Scientific discoveries could be tested and built upon in a way that made-up stories could not, and with this came a rapid acceleration of technology and accumulation of wealth and property.

It's quite fashionable for academics and activists these days to complain that progress is an illusion and that we're actually worse off now than we were in the middle ages. But that's just the stress talking, man. Modern life may be no paradise for most of us, but if you could spend a week in a medieval European city you'd soon miss our comparatively fragrant modern pollution, infomercials which would seem like spellbinding entertainment compared to what was on offer, and our sheer physical beauty—Da Fino would have been considered one of the comeliest maidens in all of Florence.

It's not progress which is the problem, after all, but our attitudes towards progress—the way we employ it—that often sucks. Our minds are evolved for life on the organic African savannah, not sharply engineered cities of angles.

However, there are plenty of techniques we can employ to make ourselves more "at home" in this psychologically alien landscape: We can try to accumulate less crap, watch less TV or spend less of our time trying to "get ahead." Blaming progress for our feelings of despair is like a heroin addict blaming his addiction on the heroin. Then again, aside from our own weakness of will, it's particularly difficult to "just say no" when everybody else around you is openly shooting junk all day long.

Other forms of peer persuasion take their toll as well: due to the nature of changes in the media we're now terrified that we're going to die in ways never imagined by people 50 years ago. Polls show that most folks consider violent crime to be an epidemic, even though there has in fact been a steady decline in violent crime over the last twenty years in the U.S. and Europe. This is because centuries after the scientific revolution, folks are still not very scientific about their feelings.

The Coen Brothers' film *No Country for Old Men* encapsulates this sentiment perfectly—it seems as if we are living in hopeless times, but it is to some degree only an illusion. Sheriff Bell's failure-of-a-hero is a tragic complement to the purely comic Dude—men who attempt to make a difference but just can't. The Dude's adversary is admittedly less malignant than Bell's (a floundering phony rather than a chilling killer), but it is also the Dude's attitude which distinguishes him; unlike the Sheriff, he has cultivated a rare and enviable facility to not expect too much from the world around him—a skill arguably more useful in modern life than mathematics.

The problem with progress, of course, is that it's all mostly external to our experience. While technology, wealth and knowledge have increased dramatically, the "fine art of living" remains stuck in the dark ages, or perhaps even the Paleolithic. Though we've scientifically made sense of a good part of the world around us, this obvious frontier remains stubbornly distant still—the inner world of the human mind. Until we figure out how to make sense of all the strands in ol' Duder's head, we're going to remain just about as anguished as our ancestors, not to mention at the mercy of increasingly complex environmental pressures that will become harder to resist and more confusing to navigate.

In the meantime, we'd all do well to emulate the Dude. That is, abide as best we can in the face of unchecked progression, and take time to enjoy the simpler things. Life is a banquet of easy pleasures. But it's the cooking, not the cutlery, which sustains us. The china, man, is not the issue here.

Given the context of the movie, it is worth noting that bowling and booze were both conceived at the very dawn of civilization—the former around 3200 B.C. in Ancient Egypt and the latter around 5300 B.C in Mesopotamia. This in mind, perhaps we should take back what we said about the Greco-Romans. Human civilization may have actually peaked much earlier.

There is a Zen story about a man riding a horse which is galloping very quickly. Another man, standing alongside the road yells at him, "Where are you going?" and the man on the horse yells back, "I don't know. Ask the horse." I think that is our situation. We are riding many horses that we cannot control. The proliferation of armaments, for instance, is a horse. We have tried our best, but we cannot control these horses. Our lives are so busy.
—Thich Nhat Hanh, *Being Peace*

Men have become the tools of their tools.
—Henry David Thoreau

What we found was that when people were pursuing leisure activities that were expensive in terms of the outside resources required—activities that demanded expensive equipment, or electricity, or other forms of energy measured in BTUs, such as power boating, driving or watching television—they were significantly *less* happy than when involved in inexpensive leisure. People were happiest when they were just talking to one another, when they gardened, knitted, or were involved in a hobby; all of these activities require few material resources, but they demand a relatively high investment of psychic energy. Leisure that uses up external resources, however, often requires less attention, and as a consequence it generally provides less memorable rewards.
—Mihaly Csikszentmihalyi, *Flow: The Psychology of Optimal Experience*

The computer can't tell you the emotional story. It can give you the exact mathematical design, but what's missing is the eyebrows.
—Frank Zappa

The Luddites of 1811 to 1813, routinely caricatured in our schools as unthinking clotheads and daft enemies of progress, were in fact breaking the machines because they correctly predicted that they would destroy the old ways of life and strip men and women of their independence.
—Tom Hodgkinson, *How to be Idle*

I had a stick of *Carefree* gum, but it didn't work. I felt pretty good while I was blowing that bubble, but as soon as the gum lost its flavor, I was back to pondering my mortality.
—Mitch Hedberg

Generations had spent their lives worrying about money so that I wouldn't have to. I didn't have to do anything.
—Mark Vonnegut, *Eden Express*

You will realize why the old folks reminisce—it is not that they are nostalgic; they are stunned. It went so quickly.
—David Mamet, *True and False*

Castillo had learned a mnemonic device for remembering the laws of thermodynamics: you can't win, things are going to get worse before they get better, who says they're going to get better.
—Thomas Pynchon, *Slow Learner*

Stone, of course, cannot be destroyed. All that can be done is move it around. But it is man's task to move things around: he must choose between doing that or doing nothing at all.
—Albert Camus, *Summer*

When a load of poor deluded sad-acts are down at the shops running up debts on their credit cards, finance ministers claim that the economy is "growing" and start celebrating. Recessions are deemed to be over the moment people start spending money they don't have on things they don't need. Consumption is synonymous with "growth" and growth is good. It's always good, wherever and whenever. Hence, clearly consumption is good, all consumption, anywhere, anytime. Judged by the logic of world economics, the death of the planet will be the zenith of human achievement, because if consumption is always good, then to consume a whole planet must be the best thing of all.
—Ben Elton, *This Other Eden*

The hurt of being alone is, of course, hardly new. But loneliness is now so widespread it has become, paradoxically, a shared experience.
—Alvin Toffler, *The Third Wave*

We are now governed not so much by growth as by growths. Ours is a society founded on proliferation, on growth which continues even though it cannot be measured against any clear goals...there is no better analogy than the metastatic process in cancer: a loss of the body's organic ground rules such that a given group of cells is able to deploy its incoercible and murderous vitality to defy genetic programming and proliferate endlessly.
—Jean Baudrillard, *The Transparency of Evil*

Both of us victims of the same twentieth-century plague. Not the Black Death this time; the Grey Life.
—Aldous Huxley, *Island*

We live in a moment of history where change is so speeded up that we begin to see the present only when it is already disappearing.
—R. D. Laing

There is more to life than increasing its speed.
—Mahatma Gandhi

All progress is based upon a universal innate desire on the part of every organism to live beyond its income.
—Samuel Butler

Civilization is a limitless multiplication of unnecessary necessities.
—Mark Twain

The Tao paradoxically means standing still and moving at the same time.
—David Rosen, *The Tao of Elvis*

It's hard to remember now that there was a bitter decade-long struggle with a lot of heroism and a tremendous resistance and dedication to try to achieve a 40-hour work week. The 40-hour week lasted a couple of years after it was achieved. By now it's an idle dream. For families now it's more like a 100-hour week, because one wage earner isn't enough for the family to survive. The achievements of the union movement, which were not unreal, are being very rapidly eroded. There's been a steady decline in real wages in the United States since 1973. That's absolutely without any historical precedent.
—Noam Chomsky, *Chronicles of Dissent*

I think I've learned exactly how the fall of man occurred in the Garden of Eden. Adam and Eve were in the Garden of Eden, and Adam said one day, "Wow, Eve, here we are, at one with nature, at one with God, we'll never age, we'll never die, and all our dreams come true the instant that we have them." And Eve said, "Yeah... it's just not enough is it?"
—Bill Hicks

I used to be with it, but then they changed what "it" was. Now what I'm with isn't it, and what's it seems weird and scary to me.
—Abe Simpson, *The Simpsons*, season 7, episode 24. Script by Brent Forrester

Without deviation from the norm, progress is not possible.
—Frank Zappa

We once had an Iron Age; after a series of intervening ages, we now live in the Age of Irony. The rapid changes of the last hundred years show us that there may be no such thing as progress; that for every step forward, we take at least one step backward.
—Wes Nisker, *Crazy Wisdom*

For every moment of triumph, for every instance of beauty, many souls must be trampled.
—Hunter S. Thompson

Eve is like the gods because she can create life. The serpent was not lying.
    The eating of the fruit proves free will and creativity is possible. Without disobedience, there can be no creativity, no progress.
—David Cooper, *God is a Verb*

People ask me, "Do you have optimism about the world?" And I say, "Yes, it's great just the way it is. And you are not going to fix it up. Nobody has ever made it any better. It is never going to be any better. This is it, so take it or leave it. You are not going to correct or improve it.
—Joseph Campbell, *The Power of Myth*

The Re-creation of the Dude

WHAT IN GOD'S HOLY NAME ARE YOU BLATHERING ABOUT?

Religion

For a movie as profane as *The Big Lebowski*, there sure are a lot of religious references in it. However, it doesn't exactly bow obediently before any of their respective altars.

A character named The Jesus is not only vulgar, egotistical and cruel, but revealed to be a pedophile as well; Walter, a militantly orthodox Jew is revealed to be a convert from Catholicism, holding on to his adopted faith only out of nostalgia for his ex-wife; On the eastern side of things, Buddhist and Taoist tropes are peppered fancifully throughout, from the Dude's performing *Chi Gung* to old bowling recordings, to executing *T'ai Chi* poses on his rug with a White Russian in hand, to a confused interpretation of the Stranger's existential ruminations ("What is that, some kind of an eastern thing?"); Islam as "otherness" is also implicit in the Gulf War framing of the film, with Saddam Hussein showing up menacingly in one of Dude's dreams and Walter flinging unsavory insults at Arabs; Atheism arguably makes an implied appearance, mocked via the German Nihilists' anti-creed; finally, full-blown Dionysian-style paganism is outwardly celebrated at Jackie Treehorn's beach party bacchanal.

Given that one of this book's aims is to help propagate Dudeism as an accepted world religion, this section plays an especially important part in this book. It's crucial for us here to address both the slippery definitions of "religion," and the purpose which we believe religion plays in the film.

First off, several people have expressed doubts about the religiosity of Dudeism, complaining that it identifies no explicit God, makes no statements about the afterlife, and includes no prophecy, miracles nor even defines any canonical religious garb. However, these qualities don't necessarily define a religion. Buddhism, Taoism and Paganism name no explicit deity; Judaism and Taoism make virtually no claims about the afterlife; Buddhism and Hinduism are basically prophecy-free; and, though not mandatory, Dudeism does in fact consider bathrobes, shorts and flip-flops to be sacred vestments.

If you place them all side-by-side, what religions all really seem to have in common is this: they offer a broad psychological framework for making sense of the maddening complexities of the world, a simplifying solution from which we extract hope and strength to deal with the great challenges of both human interaction and the greater world we live in.

Philosophies like Pragmatism or Existentialism can't really be considered religions because they are much more specific, dealing as they do with specific aspects of life. Similarly, science can't be a religion because while it explains the physical world rather well, it's currently inadequate to provide a framework for ethics, contentment or community.

On the other end of the spectrum, we might point out that some "religions" aren't actually religions themselves—Unitarian Universalism, Reform Judaism and New Age Spiritualism are so devoid of specific doctrine they might as well be considered book clubs with nice logos.

In contrast, what we generally call religion attempts to address the whole shmear—economic, sexual, moral, aesthetic, emotional, practical, and intellectual. All the what-have-you, the what-the-fuck, and the what's-the-point?

The very structure of this book provides proof that Dudeism is able to say something about everything, broken as it is into so many different aspects of human life, with essays and quotes in each chapter that suggest how Dudeism has something to say about all of them. Though true Dudeists are non-dogmatic, they employ their laidback skepticism and lightheartedness to inform and inspire a majority of their personal outlooks and actions.

Though we learned from 20th century postmodernists and scientists that there are no universal ideals or principles, Dudeism maintains that there may in fact be an ideal *attitude*. To go against this attitude is to be "un-dude," and thus uptight, unlimber, and unworldly.

One way to put it is this: the universe is, at base, stubbornly flexible, unwavering and resolute in its uncertain flow. This is of course a paradox along the lines of timeworn chestnuts like: *the only rule is there are no rules,* or *moderation in everything, including moderation,* or *I was so much older then, I'm younger than that now.*

In *The Big Lebowski*, the Dude lounges at the center of a sphere of various "isms" which roll about him as if he were inside a bowling ball. While all the other characters wear their worldviews on their sleeves, they all falsely interpret them to suit their own selfish ends—putting on *errs*, as it were. Of course, this is the way most people approach religion nowadays—not to endeavor to see the big picture, but to shut it out; not to broaden their perspectives but to focus and prune them to the point where they can be more easily manipulated and made sense of.

Dudeism strives (or strolls, rather) in the opposite direction. It sees the chaos and all the "strands" of the world as playthings to be examined, then either tossed aside or kept and placed into a growing puzzle—like an existential bag lady working on a metaphysical Ph.Dude for the University of the Universe. If a piece turns out not to fit, there's no point in trying to jam it into the bag, man. The purpose is not to accumulate accoutrements, but to engender a pattern increasingly pleasing as well as plausible.

Sounds a bit like the scientific method, doesn't it? Dudeism might in fact be considered the sloppy science of selfhood in which nothing—and/or everything—is potentially sacred.

Echoes of this cheerfully skeptical attitude already exist in many major religions: Zen Buddhism, Taoism, Midrashic Judaism, Jnana Yoga, Unitarian Universalism, and Spiritual Humanism. But most of these earnest systems of inquiry only go so far, refusing to drill further than the bedrock of hallowed ground. This is either because a) without their fundament the whole system might collapse, or b) they've fallen victim to historical dogmatic baggage and the creeping, corrupting influences of organizational behavior.

Luckily, this is unlikely to happen to Dudeism—everyone knows the difference between the *dude* and the *undude*. If you forget, all you need to do is watch the movie again. And even without a funky touchstone like *The Big Lebowski*, Dudeism can be found everywhere, if you know where to look. That's pretty much the point of this book.

In any event, people often disagree on the meanings of words and whether Dudeism is a religion or not ultimately depends on the definition of the word itself. Unfortunately, "religion" is a term almost as vague as *God*. Or *man*. Or *fuck*. Or *dude*. Have it your way, Dude. It's your roll. Ultimately, that's exactly what in God's holy name we're blathering about.

Fortunately for Dudeists in America, deciding the definition of religion for oneself is one of our basic freedoms. The Supreme Court has roundly rejected priory restraint. Hopefully there will be a day when the basic freedom to adopt any religion will be recognized in countries all over the world. Then humankind can die with a smile on our face without thinking that the good courts gypped us. If that happens, we hope Dudeism will be high in the running for laziest religion worldwide. We'd take comfort in that.

The wise man in the storm prays to God, not for safety from danger, but deliverance from fear.
—Ralph Waldo Emerson

God is a concept by which we measure our pain.
—John Lennon

The nap also has a deserved reputation for its spiritual benefits. The founders of the great world religions were dedicated nappers, and indeed, it was during their roadside dozes that their visions often came. The nap is a sort of easy version of meditation. Jesus was an idler. Buddha was definitely an idler.
—Tom Hodgkinson, *How to be Idle*

Religion is a defense against the experience of God.
—Carl Jung

I believe in using words, not fists. I believe in my outrage knowing people are living in boxes on the street. I believe in honesty. I believe in a good time. I believe in good food. I believe in sex.
—Bertrand Russell

If the gods listened to the prayers of men, all humankind would quickly perish since they constantly pray for many evils to befall one another.
—Epicurus

But who prays for Satan? Who, in eighteen centuries, has had the common humanity to pray for the one sinner that needed it most?
—Mark Twain

A passionate and committed atheism can be more religious than a weary or inadequate theism.
—Karen Armstrong, *A History of God*

All great truths begin as blasphemies.
—George Bernard Shaw

I think what went wrong with Christianity is exactly like what happens when you try to get your dog to look at something on TV. Jesus pointed at God, and everybody just stared at his finger.
—Frank Miles

The true believer can believe in a political system, in a religious doctrine, or in some social movement that combines elements of the two, but the true believer cannot truly believe in life.

A true believer may worship Jehovah, Allah, or Brahma, the supernatural beings who allegedly created all life; a true believer may slavishly adhere to a dogma designed theoretically to improve life; yet for life itself—its pleasures, wonders, and delights - he or she holds minimal regard.

Music, chess, wine, card games, attractive clothing, dancing, meditation, kites, perfume, marijuana, flirting, soccer, cheeseburgers, any expression of beauty, and any recognition of genius or individual excellence: each of those things has been severely condemned and even outlawed by one cadre of true believers or another in modern times.
—Tom Robbins, *Villa Incognito*

I'm completely in favor of the separation of Church and State. My idea is that these two institutions screw us up enough on their own, so both of them together is certain death.
—George Carlin

When it is a question of money, everybody is of the same religion.
—Voltaire

Christ died for our sins. Dare we not make his martyrdom meaningless by not committing them?
—Jules Feiffer

I would have made a good Pope.
—Richard M. Nixon

Life can be painless, provided that there is sufficient peacefulness for a dozen or so rituals to be repeated simply endlessly.
—Kurt Vonnegut, *Slapstick*

If one of the great biblical themes is that God is to be found among humble people, a parallel theme is that God is also to be found in humble places.
—Conrad Hyers, *And God Created Laughter*

Blessed are the goofballs, the crazies, for they refuse to take things seriously.
—Rick Stanley

To doubt the literal meaning of the worlds of Jesus or Moses incurs hostility from most people, but it's just a fact that if Jesus or Moses were to appear today, unidentified, with the same message he spoke many years ago, his mental stability would be challenged. This isn't because what Jesus or Moses said was untrue or because modern society is in error but simply because the route they chose to reveal to others has lost relevance and comprehensibility.
—Robert Pirsig, *Zen and the Art of Motorcycle Maintenance*

I am a deeply religious nonbeliever—this is a somewhat new kind of religion.
—Albert Einstein

All in all, the refurbished creation myth owes more to Groucho than to Karl Marx. It is a tale of hungry molecules making dinosaurs and remodeling them as ducks; also of cowboys who put to sea, quelled the world with a magnetic needle, and then wagered their genes against a mushroom cloud that knowledge was a Good Thing.
—Nigel Calder, *Timescale*

I have as much authority as the Pope. I just don't have as many people who believe it.
—George Carlin

To profess to be doing God's will is a form of megalomania.
—Joseph Prescott

A lot of Christians wear crosses around their necks. You think when Jesus comes back he ever wants to see a fucking cross? It's like going up to Jackie Onassis with a rifle pendant on.
—Bill Hicks

Why, [the religious adherent] may wonder, do I hold this set of convictions rather than that set? Is it because I surveyed all the world's faiths and chose the one whose claims seemed most convincing? Almost certainly not. If you have a faith, it is statistically overwhelmingly likely that it is the same faith as your parents and grandparents had.
—Richard Dawkins, *Virus of the Mind*

God is never so fashionable as during wartime. Even the atheist society of the Soviet Union, during the ravages of the Second World War, found it necessary to reinstate God temporarily to assure full sacrifice on the part of its citizens.
—Robert Ardrey, *African Genesis*

Throughout history power has been the vice of the ascetic.
—Bertrand Russell

Is God willing to prevent evil, but not able?
Then he is not omnipotent.
Is he able, but not willing?
Then he is malevolent.
Is he both able and willing?
Then whence cometh evil?
Is he neither able nor willing?
Then why call him God?
—Epicurus

If we take eternity to mean not infinite temporal duration but timelessness, then eternal life belongs to those who live in the present.
—Ludwig Wittgenstein

Every honest man is a Prophet; he utters his opinion both of Private and Public matters. Thus: if you go on so, the result is so.
—William Blake

People don't come to church for preachments, of course, but to daydream about God.
—Kurt Vonnegut, *Palm Sunday*

A cult is a religion with no political power.
—Tom Wolfe, *In Our Time*

Religion is to do right. It is to love, it is to serve, it is to think, it is to be humble.
—Ralph Waldo Emerson

The great enemy of religion is not godlessness so much as…apathy, dullness, passivity and boredom.
—Conrad Hyers, *And God Created Laughter*

In the sixteenth century human life was disordered and talent stultified by the obsession of theology; today we are plague-stricken by politics.
—Evelyn Waugh, *When the Going Was Good*

Hell has no power over pagans.
—Arthur Rimbaud, *A Season in Hell*

The writer Thomas Berry says that it's all a question of story. The story is the plot we assign to life and the universe, our basic assumptions and fundamental beliefs about how things work. He says we are in trouble now "because we are between stories. The old story sustained us for a long time—it shaped our emotional attitudes, it provided us with life's purpose...Everything was taken care of because the story was there. Now the story is not functioning. And we have not learned a new."
—Joseph Campbell, *The Power of Myth*

Who would think by looking at pictures of the Crucifixion in a cathedral that the essence of Christianity is love?
—Rick Gore, *"People Like Us," National Geographic Magazine*, July 2000

Any system built on belief functions through the operations of guilt and hypocrisy.
—David Mamet, *True and False*

Characters will serve till Messiah comes, characters whose powerful existence in our minds makes a real-life messiah unnecessary. Imperfect, even childish human beings, writers raise themselves up by the techniques of fiction to something much better than even the best writers are in everyday life: ordinary mortals transmuted for the moment into apostles.
—John Gardner, *On Writers and Writing*

What's Your Drink?

CAREFUL, MAN, THERE'S A BEVERAGE HERE

Spirits

Though the Judeo-Christian biblical record can read like one giant acid flashback at times, it can also be argued that it is an accurate record of history, albeit couched in cinematic fairy tale imagery. The Garden of Eden, for instance, can be interpreted not as a bizarre creation fantasy, but as a nostalgia for a time before agriculture, when human life was relatively relaxed, animals were our friends, and clothing was optional.

In fact, hunting and gathering and animal husbandry were pretty groovy lifestyles, offering lots of travel, healthy grub, and less effort overall than agriculture. So what impelled man to suddenly put up stakes and grow grain instead?

There would have had to be a good reason—wheat is not as tasty as meat, nor is it as healthy as vegetables and roots. Plus, it's much less fortifying to rely on a single foodstuff, and dangerous too—staying in one place with all that food makes you an easy target for marauders.

What's worse, protecting your crops from outsiders and shepherds tends to turn you into a human paraquat—the biblical Cain and Abel story (which immediately follows the one about Eden) illustrates this perfectly.

According to the story, Cain killed his brother Abel because he was jealous that God said he preferred Abel's kebabs to his own handmade pita bread. However, if history is anything to go by, Cain killed Abel for a far more simple reason: because Abel's goats were eating all his crops. Once agriculture got up and running, landed farmers would not tolerate freewheeling shepherds wandering into their territory and quickly began killing them off. Across this line, you do not graze.

In all fairness, we might forgive Cain on the grounds of chronic drunkenness. That's because one of the most plausible reasons why humans stopped hunting, gathering, and shepherding in order to sit around and raise grain is because of beer.

That's right, dude. Oat soda. The *weitzen*. Once our distant ancestors found out that wheat left alone for long enough under the right conditions will produce a mind-limbering brew, they were forced to wait around for fermentation to perform its magic. And they needed wheat. Lots of it. Then their fucking troubles were over. For a few hours at a time.

It's no coincidence that the dawn of civilization occurred around 5200 B.C., precisely the moment the first evidence of beer-manufacture makes its appearance. Evidently, Mesopotamia became a hard place to leave as a result. This might help explain why today it's only that part of the world (the Middle East) that doesn't drink a lot of booze anymore; they long ago had their fill and moved on to hashish.

Beer was a big part of this first civilization, so much so that the inhabitants sang its praises in verse. The Sumerians, as the people of this civilization are now known, produced the world's first written epic story, the Epic of Gilgamesh in which the ruler of civilization (Gilgamesh) needs to civilize Enkidu, a powerful wild man who lives outside the city walls. The magic, civilizing elixir he employs to tame him? Beer, naturally. After sharing several pitchers, they become the best of friends and join forces against evil. This is currently the oldest story known to mankind.

If the Epic of Gilgamesh is anything to go by, alcohol is not only the cause of civilization, but has been its preserver from the beginning—binding humans together in brotherly and sisterly solidarity. If there's anything that Dudeism stands for above all, it's the value of friendly good feeling and the art of skillful relaxation. In this, alcohol stands as a very welcome (but not mandatory) sacrament, a means to fraternal ends and league play.

Though the Dude orders beer from time to time during the course of the movie, he generally prefers a much more curious and complex beverage—the White Russian. It's an odd choice for a deeply casual and unassuming fellow—creamy and sweet, it is a drink more often favored by young ladies than shabby middle-aged layabouts like the Dude.

It's been said that you are what you eat, but "you are what you drink" might be a more apropos axiom. Coffee or tea? Beer or wine? Bourbon or banana liqueur? These questions surely say more about you than light meat or dark, French fries or onion rings, surf or turf. So, then, what does the White Russian say about the Dude?

First off, it says he's not macho. Far from it. That's Walter's thing. The Dude has no problems indulging his feminine side—how many modern fellows take baths with scented candles? Or are concerned enough about their home décor enough to chase down a missing rug? What's more, he barely fights back when challenged. Though tough guys might accordingly refer to him by a certain term for a part of the female anatomy (vagina), he wouldn't bat an eye in response. The word does not make him the least bit uncomfortable.

Secondly, his drink of choice might be a sly nod to the Cold War. "White Russians" were the anti-communist forces during the Russian revolution. In 1949 the Black Russian cocktail was created as a dig at that nation, at that time loathed and feared by the West. With all the "hot" war references in the film (Korea, Vietnam, WWII, the Gulf War), it's only fair that the cold war got some attention too.

Finally, the Dude, with his Polish/Russian surname, may be fancifully honoring his ethnic heritage with the beverage. Note that he also calls the drink a "Caucasian," and that the Caucasus mountain range, formerly believed to be the homeland of the Caucasians (the whites) in fact wends its way through southern Russia. One wonders—in a place like Los Angeles, with its sea of ethnic migrants and froth of personal reinvention, it might just be that the Dude is reluctant to let go of this silly, superficial shrine to his ethnic heritage. The Dude is then, to some degree, a White Russian. You are what you drink.

Nevertheless, whatever the Dude's personal choice of cocktail, it's his attitude and purpose in imbibing it that illuminates his character. Though people often drink to forget, they just as often drink to the honor of something or someone—that is, to remember. The Dude drinks not to escape the world, but to embellish it, to toast the tree of life. *Aitz Chaim He*, as Walter mentioned his ex used to say—quite literally apropos of nothing.

Therefore it's no wonder he takes such umbrage at nearly being made to spill his drink by a zealous flunky of the Big Lebowski—"Careful, man! There's a beverage here" the Dude exclaims. His cocktail is a jolly, holy sacrament and must be honored. One of the sacred Dudeist commandments must be *Thou shall not spill*. After all, it was upon such a life-altering elixir the foundations of civilization have been built. It is one of the only decent things we received, it seems, in exchange for Eden.

Always carry a flagon of whiskey in case of snakebite and furthermore always carry a small snake.
—W.C. Fields

Alcohol! The cause of, and solution to, all of life's problems.
—Homer Simpson, *The Simpsons,* Season 8, Episode 18. Script by John Swartzwelder

Beer and wine making are among civilization's earliest professions. One of the most common pictographs in Sumerian ruins is the sign for beer—hatch marks that represent the crisscross patterns dug into the bottom of beer vessels.
—Stephen Braun, *Buzz*

My doctor tells me I should start slowing it down—but there are more old drunks than there are old doctors so let's all have another round.
—Willie Nelson

He was a wise man who invented beer.
—Plato

Yes she drank alone. You bet. And why did she drink alone? Because she was *alone*.
—Martin Amis, *London Fields*

Prior to the introduction of the potato, beer was second only to bread as the main source of nourishment for most central and north Europeans.
    ...An English family in the latter half of the seventeenth century—the period when coffee drinking was catching on among the upper classes—consumed about three liters of beer per person daily, children included.
—Wolfgang Schivelbusch, *Tastes of Paradise*

Alcohol is the anesthesia by which we endure the operation of life.
—George Bernard Shaw

Champagne, if you are seeking the truth, is better than a lie detector. It encourages a man to be expansive, even reckless, while lie detectors are only a challenge to tell lies successfully.
—Graham Greene

Even though a number of people have tried, no one has yet found a way to drink for a living.
—Jean Kerr

I'd rather have a bottle in front o' me than a frontal lobotomy.
—Tom Waits

Religions change; beer and wine remain.
—Harvey Allen

It's my theory that everybody would be a drunk if they could bear to get that way. We'd all feel so much better if we were drunk all the time. But it's very hard getting to be a drunk. Only drunks seem to be able to manage it.
—Martin Amis, *Other People*

After spending the day either living in the past (regrets, reports) or in the future (anxieties, Powerpoint presentations), the first drink of the day brings us into the present moment: we become Buddhists.
—Tom Hodgkinson, *How to be Idle*

I believe, if we take habitual drunkards as a class, their heads and their hearts will bear an advantageous comparison with those of any other class.
—Abraham Lincoln

Work is the curse of the drinking classes.
—Oscar Wilde

Once they came to understand this simple beer-making process and were able to repeat it successfully, the Stone Age people of the late Neolithic period abandoned their nomadic lifestyle to become farmers of grain in order to make their favorite beverage…Thus began the civilization of man.
—*Mental Floss Magazine*, November 2001

The most important thing to remember about drunks is that drunks are far more intelligent than non-drunks. They spend a lot of time talking in pubs, unlike workaholics who concentrate on their careers and ambitions, who never develop their higher spiritual values, who never explore the insides of their head like a drunk does.
—Shane MacGowan

All adventures begin with drink. And all end with women.
—Soseki Natsume

You can't be a real country unless you have a beer and an airline. It helps if you have some kind of a football team, or some nuclear weapons, but at the very least you need a beer.
—Frank Zappa

Claude Levi-Strauss makes out a good case for the invention of mead as a passage from "nature to culture," a process defining human behavior.
—Maguelonne Toussaint-Samat, *History of Food*

Man being reasonable must get drunk.
—Lord Byron

Be always drunken…Drunken with what? With wine, with poetry, or with virtue, as you will. But be drunken.
—Charles Baudelaire

Beer is proof that God loves us and wants us to be happy.
—Benjamin Franklin

In fact the ancient world did not see intoxication, whether induced by mead, beer or diluted wine, as reprehensible. To some extent it was regarded as an act of religion in the literal sense of the word, creating a bond between man and God, like the use of drugs by the Amerindians and some oriental sects to liberate the divinity hidden within every human soul in ecstasy. Given a good head, you could feel the god within you. The Greek term for ritual intoxication was enthousiasmous, divine possesion. The veneration of Dionysus went hand in hand with this.
—Maguelonne Toussaint-Samat, *History of Food*

In wine there is wisdom, in beer there is freedom…in water there is bacteria.
—Benjamin Franklin

Distilling is beautiful. First of all because it is a slow, philosophic and silent occupation, which keeps you busy but gives you time to think of other things, somewhat like riding a bike. Then, because it involves a metamorphosis from liquid to vapor (invisible), and from this once again to liquid; but in this double journey, up and down, purity is attained…And finally, when you set about distilling, you acquire the consciousness of repeating a ritual consecrated by the centuries, almost a religious act, in which from imperfect material you obtain the essence, the *usia*, the spirit, and in the first place alcohol, which gladdens the spirit and warms the heart.
—Primo Levi, *The Periodic Table*

The secret of drunkenness is that it insulates us in thought, whilst it unites us in feeling.
—Ralph Waldo Emerson

Drunkenness is temporary suicide.
—Bertrand Russell

[Donald] Goodwin estimates that at least a third of twentieth-century American writers of stature were or are alcoholics by current reasonable definition, and that over seventy percent of American Nobel laureates in literature have been alcoholic as well.
—Melvin Konner, *Why the Reckless Survive*

The womb, the teats, nipples, breast-milk, tears, laughter.
—Walt Whitman

I drink so I
can talk to assholes.
This includes me.
—Jim Morrison, *Wilderness*

Be thou from Hell upsprung or Heaven descended,
Beauty! Thy look demoniac and divine
Pours good and evil things confusedly blended,
And therefore are thou likened unto wine.
—Charles Baudelaire, *Hymn to Beauty*

Good God, what does it matter? If life is a tragedy, or a farce, or a disaster, or anything else, what do I care! Let life be what it likes. Give me a drink, that is what I want just now.
—D.H. Lawrence, *"Herman Melville's Typee and Omoo"*

Far Out

A PRETTY STRICT, UH, DRUG UH, REGIMEN

Drugs

It's hard to believe it now, but there once was a time when virtually all drugs were not only legal, they were a highly sought-after supplement regularly indulged in by the elites of Europe and America. Narcotics like laudanum, opium, hashish and cocaine were easily obtainable without a prescription—provided you could afford them. If modern politicians are to be believed, civilization should have collapsed in a heap right then and there.

Presumably, however, the rich can handle their drugs. It was only in the early 20th century, by which the teeming masses had grown wealthy enough to purchase these wonders of medical mood-enhancement that authorities started to clamp down. It was all fine and dandy for dukes and earls to ease their days with something stronger than gin, but in the hands of the intemperate hordes, drug usage was reckoned too risky. As the market opened up, pharmacies narrowed their gates and over the course of the century, one narcotic, amphetamine, barbiturate and hallucinogen after another was either hidden under the counter, or banned entirely.

This is where we are today, much to the detriment of the quality of our lives as well as our much-lauded "freedoms." Like children, we are not to be trusted near the cookie jar.

The problem is, of course, we're not children, and most of the cookies aren't nearly as dangerous as driving a car. It's as if policymakers all over the world got together to read Alice in Wonderland and decided it was a true story. Rabbit holes beneath our feet were set to open up everywhere!

The concern, as we all know, is that drugs make people lose control of their lives and to offer unfettered access to them would result in a collapse of ordered society. Only, there's absolutely no evidence to suggest this would ever happen.

Outside of severe hallucinogens like PCP, by far the most "dangerous" drug of all is alcohol, and aside from the fistfights, car accidents and karaoke it causes, society still celebrates it. Marijuana, on the other hand, may well be the only drug in the world under the influence of which no one has ever died—there is literally not a single documented case. Yet hundreds of people die from aspirin overdoses every year. Truly everything in your house is more dangerous than dope: vastly more people are hurt each year from being hit by pots than they are from taking hits of pot. Should crockery be contraband?

Aside from making you lazy and a little forgetful, the only really negative side effect of dope is an infantilization of taste: e.g. a fondness for Hostess-brand snack cakes, Saturday Morning Cartoons, interminable drum circles and bands that consider the didgeridoo a musical instrument.

Then there's the argument about marijuana being a "gateway drug" that leads to other, harder drugs. This is as specious an argument as suggesting that jaywalking is a "gateway" crime that leads to robbery and murder. True, people who rob and kill are probably more likely to jaywalk as well, but the vast majority of citizens know how far they can reasonably expose themselves and others to danger. In other words, very few recreational tokers are likely to trade in their hash pipe for a crack pipe. One might as well deem booze and cigarettes gateway drugs because the majority of crackheads started smoking and drinking before anything else.

Though other drugs invite varying degrees of actual danger into their users' lives, nearly all of the actual hazards involve the purchase of the drug from illicit sources. Overdoses of heroin generally occur not because people keep upping the dosage but because of the great variability in quality and strength between doses—being unregulated, it's difficult to know for sure how much you're taking. If heroin were legalized and standardized the way pharmaceuticals were, heroin-related deaths would be overwhelmingly reduced. Furthermore, smack would be cheap enough that people wouldn't have to rob, kill and whore themselves in order to afford it.

Does "easy drugs for everyone" sound like a marketing strategy to push the apocalypse? Don't worry, the danger of attracting new addicts is minor: For instance, pharmaceuticals are cheap and relatively easy to obtain, and outside of a few high-profile actors, people rarely become Vicodin addicts. And as anyone who's ever had surgery knows, Vicodin is awesome.

Then there are drugs like ecstasy and LSD, which many very scholarly, upstanding members of society have felt would provide tremendous benefit in helping the brain and our emotions experience their full potential. Taken in comfortable surroundings under the supervision of trained professionals, drugs like these have literally changed peoples' lives in a way that ten-plus years of expensive psychotherapy rarely do.

The bottom line is this: not only are most drugs not really dangerous, but people are better able to make decisions for themselves about drugs than our policymakers think. As P.J. O'Rourke once put it, "getting fucked up is for those who are already fucked up." That is, people who lose themselves on drugs almost surely have problems that are more profound than the drugs themselves. And they'll get drugs anyhow, so why not provide them with a less-risky means to get them? Throw in some free counseling if you like—society will be far better off if drug use isn't delegated to the dark corners.

Like most people we know, the Dude doesn't have a problem with drugs—he smokes joints now and then and does throw back a few drinks a day but he's not compulsive about it. And other than "the occasional acid flashback" he's not rooting around for wilder, hairier experiences. And so what if he was? When it comes to serving up a brain cell soufflé, most people clearly know the difference between nicely baked and burnt to a crisp.

Furthermore, a close examination of the Dude's behavior shows that he gets high on lots of other things than mere drugs: From serenely performing an *ad hoc* Tai Chi on his replacement rug, to experiencing ecstasy while listening to a Creedence song to goofily sniffing the carton of half-and-half at the supermarket and then skipping home elfin-like, most everything the Dude does is done with ginger aplomb and a lightness of step—even at times when he's carrying the weight of the world on his shoulders.

Unlike other obsessive characters in the film, life for the Dude is a constant trip, a perennial source of amusement, a string of semi-connected "far out" moments.

When the nihilists violently break into his house and start smashing his personal belongings, only the Dude could delightedly and distractedly coo "nice marmot" just before they sic the untamed animal upon his Johnson. Only the Dude could find so many people with such varied backgrounds so "fucking interesting." And only the Dude can consider audio recordings of bowling tournaments four years prior suitable meditation material. Finally, when it comes to being unconscious, no one dreams quite like the Dude.

It's often said that drugs don't put anything there that isn't already in front of you; they just help you see them more clearly. There's no doubt that someday what we call "drugs" will be considered "supplements" and will be unlawful as a latte. Until then, those looking to abide by the letter of the law might opt to watch *The Big Lebowski* and try looking at the world through the Dude's eyes.

Just don't do it too many times or you too might get addicted. Currently there is no detox program for we truly dedicated Dudeheads.

No drug, not even alcohol, causes the fundamental ills of society. If we're looking for the source of our troubles, we shouldn't test people for drugs, we should test them for stupidity, ignorance, greed and love of power.
—P.J. O'Rourke, *Give War a Chance*

I've never had a problem with drugs. I've had problems with the police.
—Keith Richards

The other day they asked me about mandatory drug testing. I said I believed in drug testing a long time ago. All through the sixties I tested everything.
—Bill "Spaceman" Lee

The whole subject of pleasure triggers intense controversy. Should pleasure come as a reward for work or suffering? Should people feel guilty if they experience pleasure without suffering for it in some way? Should work itself be unpleasant? These questions are very important to us, but they do not have easy answers. Different people and different cultures answer them in different ways...

Drug use is universal. Every human culture in every age of history has used one or more psychoactive drugs. (The one exception is the Eskimos, who were unable to grow drug plants and had to wait for white men to bring them alcohol.) In fact, drug taking is so common that it seems to be a basic human activity.
—Andrew Weil, Winifred Rosen, *Chocolate to Morphine*

The best mind-altering drug is truth.
—Lily Tomlin

The question arises, therefore, why cannabis is so regularly banned in countries where alcohol is permitted...It may be that we can ban cannabis simply because the people who use it, or would do so, carry little weight in social matters and are relatively easy to control, whereas the alcohol user often carries plenty of weight in social matters and is difficult to control, as the U.S. prohibition era showed. It has yet to be shown, however, that the one is more socially or personally disruptive than the other.
—Henry B.M Murphy, M.D

They lie about marijuana. Tell you pot-smoking makes you unmotivated. Lie! When you're high, you can do everything you normally do, just as well. You just realize that it's not worth the fucking effort. There is a difference.
—Bill Hicks

I'm not pro-drug. They obviously cause a lot of damage. But I am pro-logic, and you're never going to stop the human need for release through altered consciousness. The government could take away all the drugs in the world, and people would spin around on their lawn until they fell down and saw God.
—Dennis Miller

Did you know America ranks the lowest in education but the highest in drug use? It's nice to be number one, but we can fix that. All we need to do is start the war on education. If it's anywhere near as successful as our war on drugs, in no time we'll all be hooked on phonics.
—Leighann Lord

The taboo on narcotics (opium, hashish, marijuana, cocaine, heroin, morphine, etc.) and their being made illegal in today's world happened fairly recently. Until the end of the nineteenth century narcotics were treated and used in a laissez-faire manner.
—Wolfgang Schivelbusch, *Tastes of Paradise*

Reality is a crutch for people who can't cope with drugs.
—Lily Tomlin

Of course, nondrug highs can present the same problems. People who are dependent on falling in love for their highs are equally at the mercy of outside forces. Many individuals get a rush from making money, and their lives are consumed in its pursuit. We have seen fanatical joggers who experience severe mental and physical discomfort if circumstances prevent them from running for even a day—a kind of withdrawal syndrome painful to them and those around them. If the only effective way you have of getting high is downhill skiing or hang gliding, you are going to have to spend as much time and money getting high as any serious drug user, and you will expose yourself to equal or greater physical risk. There are men who get their greatest highs from killing; some of them find acceptable roles in society as professional soldiers, others become criminals and terrorists.

    The goal should be to learn how to get high in ways that do not hurt yourself or others, and that do not necessarily require huge expenditures of time or money for special materials and equipment. Furthermore, you should be able to get high in enough different ways so that you can have the experience wherever you are, even if your external resources are minimal. You should also be willing to experiment with new methods of getting high as you mature and change.
—Andrew Weil, Winifred Rosen, *Chocolate to Morphine*

I was high on life, but eventually I built up a tolerance.
—Arj Barker

Everything is a drug; it depends on the dose.
—Paracelsus

Drugs have taught an entire generation of American kids the metric system.
—P.J. O'Rourke, *The CEO of the Sofa*

Now they're calling drugs an epidemic. That's because white folks are doing it.
—Richard Pryor

The War on Drugs is a big waste of money. The government is pissing it away just so they can put on a big show for the people who are against drugs, because those people happen to vote. I don't think marijuana smokers get to the voting booth as often as they'd like to. "What, it was yesterday?"
—Drew Carey

Every now and then when your life gets complicated and the weasels start closing in, the only cure is to load up on heinous chemicals and then drive like a bastard from Hollywood to Las Vegas…with the music at top volume and at least a pint of ether.
—Hunter S Thompson

I used to do drugs. I still do drugs. But I used to, too.
—Mitch Hedberg

The basic thing nobody asks is why do people take drugs of any sort? Why do we have these accessories to normal living to live? I mean, is there something wrong with society that's making us so pressurized, that we cannot live without guarding ourselves against it?
—John Lennon

Annual drug deaths: tobacco: 395,000, alcohol: 125,000; "legal drugs": 38,000, illegal drug overdoses: 5,200, marijuana, 0. Considering government subsidies of tobacco, just what is our government protecting us from in the drug war?
—William A. Turnbow

I have never seen two people on pot get in a fight because it is fucking IMPOSSIBLE. "Hey, buddy!" "Hey, what?" "Ummmmmmm…." End of argument.
—Bill Hicks

A surprisingly good case could be made that much of culture is hallucination. The whole intent and function of ritual appears to be a group wish to hallucinate reality.
—Weston La Barre

Nobody stopped thinking about those psychedelic experiences. Once you've been to some of those places, you think, "How can I get back there again but make it a little easier on myself?"
—Jerry Garcia

That humanity at large will ever be able to dispense with Artificial Paradises seems very unlikely. Most men and women lead lives at the worst so painful, at the best so monotonous, poor and limited that the urge to escape, the longing to transcend themselves if only for a few moments, is and has always been one of the principal appetites for the soul. Art and religion, carnivals and saturnalia, dancing and listening to oratory—all these have served, in H.G. Wells' phrase, as Doors in the Wall. And for private, for everyday use there have always been chemical intoxicants. All the vegetable sedatives and narcotics, all the euphorics that grow on trees, the hallucinogens that ripen in berries or can be squeezed from roots—all, without exception, have been known and systematically used by human beings from time immemorial. And to these natural modifiers of consciousness modern science has added its quota of synthetics.

We now spend a good deal more on drink and smoke than we spend on education. This, of course, is not surprising. The urge to escape from selfhood and the environment is in almost everyone almost all the time. The urge to do something for the young is strong only in parents, and in them only for the few years during which their children go to school.
—Aldous Huxley, The Doors of Perception

If you don't believe drugs have done good things for us, then go home and burn all your records, all your tapes, and all your CDs because every one of those artists who have made brilliant music and enhanced your lives? RrrrrrrrrrrrrrrrrrrEAL fucking high on drugs. The Beatles were so fucking high they let Ringo sing a few songs.
—Bill Hicks

Over time, a drug user needs a progressively larger dose to produce an equivalent level of exhilaration; similarly, our civilization seems to require an ever-increasing level of consumption. But why do we assume that it's natural and normal for our per capita consumption of most natural resources to increase every year? Do we need higher levels of consumption to achieve the same distracting effect once produced by a small amount of consumption?...are we sometimes less interested in a careful balancing of the pros and cons than in the great thrill sure to accompany the first use of the new enhancement of human power over the earth?
—Al Gore, Earth in the Balance

Music is a safe type of high. It's more the way it was supposed to be. That's where highness came, I guess, from anyway. It's nothing but rhythm and motion.
—Jimi Hendrix

The more people smoke herb, the more Babylon fall.
—Bob Marley

Before all else, people use music for mood-enhancement. Psychologists have long known that different personality types are attracted to different kinds of drugs, legal and illegal. There's a parallel here. We "take" a certain kind of music to steer our central nervous systems toward a particular condition: hard rock as the frenzied rush of cocaine; easy-listening genres as a martini; cheery supermarket Musak as a pick-me-up of coffee; cool jazz as a laid-back marijuana high; the far-flung landscapes of classical music as the fantasy realm of psychedelics.
—Robert Jourdain, *Music, the Brain, & Ecstasy*

No, I don't do drugs anymore, either. But I'll tell you something about drugs. I used to do drugs, but I'll tell you something honestly about drugs, honestly, and I know it's not a very popular idea, you don't hear it very often anymore, but it is the truth: I had a great time doing drugs. Sorry. Never murdered anyone, never robbed anyone, never raped anyone, never beat anyone, never lost a job, a car, a house, a wife or kids, laughed my ass off, and went about my day.
—Bill Hicks

The sun is so bright that the stars are invisible, despite the fact that they are just as present in the sky at daytime as at night. When the sun sets, we are able to perceive the stars. In the same way, the brilliance of our most recent evolutionary accretion, the verbal abilities of the left hemisphere, obscures our awareness of the functions of the intuitive right hemisphere, which in our ancestors must have been the principal means of perceiving the world.
    Marijuana is often described as improving our appreciation of and abilities in music, dance, art, pattern and sign recognition, and our sensitivity to nonverbal communication. I wonder if, rather than enhancing anything, the cannibinols simply suppress the left hemisphere and permit the stars to come out. This may also be the objective of the meditative states of many Oriental religions.
—Carl Sagan, *The Dragons of Eden*

Student: What is the nature of Buddha?
Ts'ao-shan: Three pounds of hemp!
—*The Gateless Gate*

It was said that women could not be given the vote, and that kings could not give up absolute power, because society would disintegrate. The same is said about legalizing drugs today.
—Terence McKenna, *Food of the Gods*

The right to chew or smoke a plant that grows wild in nature, such as hemp, is anterior to and more basic than the right to vote.
—Thomas Szasz, *Our Right to Drugs*

Perhaps to some extent we have lost sight of the fact that LSD can be very, very helpful in our society if used properly.
—Senator Robert Kennedy, *Subcommittee on Executive Reorganization, 1966*

Pygmies prepare themselves for the hunt through marijuana intoxication, allowing them the patience to wait for long hours. Pot is their only cultivated crop. It would be interesting if in human history the cultivation of marijuana led to the invention of agriculture and thereby to civilization.
—Carl Sagan, *The Dragons of Eden*

The future is going to spin faster, and wilder, of that we can be sure. If you don't like acid, rest assured you're not going to like the future. Now, more than ever before, we need to gear our brains to multiplicity, complexity, relativity, change. Those who can handle acid will be able to deal joyfully with what is to come.
—Timothy Leary

Wine makes a man good-natured and sociable; hashish isolates him. The one is industrious, as it were; the other, essentially lazy. Indeed, what point is there in working, toiling, writing, creating anything at all, when it is possible to obtain Paradise in a single swallow?
—Charles Baudelaire, *Artifical Paradise*

But before I rise, man, why not roll still another one, to make sure I'm really stoned, because sometimes, man, in my condition, it is hard to tell.
—William Kotzwinkle, *The Fan Man*

174 – The Sexes

You mean, coitus?

STRONGLY VAGINAL, AND A PAIR OF TESTICLES

The Sexes

As you may have surmised from this book, *The Big Lebowski* is pretty fertile ground for highfalutin' discussion. But there's stuff out there far more complex even than what you've found in the pages of this far-reaching, rambling, and occasionally ridiculous collection of essays.

An academic symposium in fact took place several years back during a Lebowskifest[8] in which papers were submitted with titles like "The Big Lebowski as Medieval Grail-Quest" and "The Big Lebowski and Paul de Man: Historicizing Irony and Ironizing Historicism"—most of which were published to wide acclaim in the book *The Year's Work in Lebowski Studies*. Several other scholarly lebookskis followed, including our own *Lebowski 101*. If the trend continues, someday universities might even be awarding Ph.Dude degrees in Lebowski studies. In fact, we're about to do just that at our very own Abide University[9].

As these collections of philosophical investigations into the film suggest, *The Big Lebowski* can inform even the most unlikely subjects. Given that the film concerns mostly male characters it might come as a surprise that many academics have interpreted it as a movie about feminism. And yet, as the Stranger puts it "there is no bottom"—*The Big Lebowski* is about everything.

Several of these scholars have made strong arguments that *The Big Lebowski*'s primary concern is the emasculation and increasing obsolescence of the contemporary American male. The argument goes like this: Now that we live in a society in which women are free to earn commensurable salaries as men, and to live as liberally as men have long been accustomed to, the male role as protector and provider has become very drastically scaled back in importance. As the Dude puts it, what makes a man

---

[8] www.lebowskifest.com
[99] www.aui.me

these days is not heroism, but simply a "pair of testicles"—or rather the sperm generated to help perpetuate the species. Just about everything else can be handled adequately by women. Except maybe for really awesome guitar solos. For some reason women just don't seem able to pull those off convincingly. (Note: This is not sexism—it is a fact even female rocker P.J. Harvey openly concedes. Men can't give birth, women can't shred. Life isn't fair.)

Thus, if all men except, say, Strato-master Yngwie Malmsteen were to drop dead tomorrow, women and sperm banks could keep mankind going on for just about ever.

The main characters deal with this crisis of identity in different ways: Walter by asserting masculine calls-to-arms, even when warfare is clearly unnecessary; the Big Lebowski by faking competence, largesse, and competent governance of his household; the Dude by opting out of all domestic, reproductive and professional roles entirely; and already-invisible Donnie by feebly and unaccountably dropping dead.

Other characters evince their male irrelevance in more subtle manners: Once prolific writer of war stories Arthur Digby Sellers is now mute, muzzled by an iron lung; The Jesus diverts his outlandish sexual energy into pedophilia; the Nihilists self-consciously insist they don't care about anything, even though they desperately do; porn mogul Jackie Treehorn is not only suffering a downward arc in the sex industry, but has been outsmarted by one of his ingénues; finally, even that greatest of all macho American figures, the cowboy (represented by the Stranger) seems as if he might have given up roping fillies and is now digging stylish fellers like the Dude instead.

The women in the film, on the other hand, are uniformly powerful, clever and dominating. Maude, her unnamed mother, Bunny, and Walter's ex-wife Cynthia all effortlessly manipulate the men in their lives.

The Big Lebowski is revealed to have been left no money of his own by his dead wife, he receives no respect from their daughter Maude, and his young porn star wife cheats on him openly. Echoing the same brash, overcompensating demeanor of the Big Lebowski, militant Walter turns out to have his manhood wrapped around the finger of his ex—obediently taking care of her dog while she's on vacation with another man, and bathetically clinging to the Orthodox Judaism he converted to when he married her.

Of course, the characters in the film exhibit extreme cases. Our own situations aren't generally so dire: though modern male roles are being reformulated, guys aren't necessarily in a state of panic over it. If anything, the changing landscape of domestic relationships and occupational roles means that, like women, men too enjoy far greater freedom now to untie themselves from the traditional expectations of society. And this is one of the principal things that makes the Dude such a compelling, idealized character to many men—he is living the dream life many modern males might downwardly aspire to were they not deeply inculcated with conventional moral codes.

As a society, we too often assume that all men want to wield power and wealth, that they want to raise families and sire noble offspring, that they want to be admired by their peers as they strut down the street, and that they want to work hard for a cause or a company, to make a difference in the world. Yet these imperatives are not necessarily inherent in the male psyche. Rather, they are more likely gleaned from a few thousand years of civilization. Evolutionary Psychology tells a different story about the lifestyle we're evolved to lead.

The way we lived for millennia on the African savannah, in which our inner emotional architecture was formed, was most probably this: We hung out in small tribes of friends. Monogamy was rare—instead just about everybody got to swap sexual partners. True, the alpha males got most of the action, but the betas and gammas probably got laid more then than they do today. Children were reared by the group—primarily by the females. Men hung out together during weeks-long hunting trips and bonded while the women stayed at home and foraged for vegetables and tubers. There was little competition between the males within the group because everyone knew where they stood in a loosely-defined hierarchy of dominance. Discord and competition took place primarily when interlopers from alien tribes contested or coveted hunting lands. Otherwise, things were probably pretty hunky dory and as close to pastoral paradise as medieval painters ever imagined, if considerably more filthy.

The Dude's attitude, then, is a bit of a throwback to that halcyon era. He's not looking to get married, get a job, play one-upmanship with other men, nor accumulate wealth, social status or possessions. He's essentially got a stone-age mind, which is not as bad a thing as it sounds: African pygmies live much the same way today, and cultural anthropologists have repeatedly held them up as an example of a primitive society in many ways preferable to our own. Moreover, their easygoing way of life may even have been aided by a long association with marijuana, possibly even stretching back to prehistoric times (a theory espoused by Great Dude in History Carl Sagan). Thus, the "stone age" could well have been the stoner age as well, and a pretty golden one at that.

After all this, it's a shame that Dudeism tends to resonate more with men than with women—in trying to be more like "traditional" guys, women are now prone to suffer the same stresses and struggles that men have had to contend with over these last centuries.

Hopefully these newly-empowered ladies won't overlook the value of just taking 'er easy, hanging out with their buddies, getting limber, and walking around in their underpants—after all, that does describe the less bitchy scenes of *Sex and the City*. Only, instead of obsessing over pricey footwear like those women, we suggest they entertain the perennial allure of cheapo flip-flops and the transcendent, translucent jelly sandal.

We cannot expect too much from the human capacity to reason, anyway, since its most elaborate energy is channeled as a rule into self-delusion and its most imposing construction erected so far has been that fairy-tale tower, the romantic fallacy.
—Robert Ardrey, *African Genesis*

The mating rituals of great cats and many other animals are barely distinguishable, in their early stages, from fighting.
—Carl Sagan, *The Dragons of Eden*

The betrothed and accepted lover has lost the wildest charms of his maiden by her acceptance. She was heaven while he pursued her, but she cannot be heaven if she stoops to one such as he!
—Ralph Waldo Emerson

As the history of war is in large part the story of peoples who will risk all for release from boredom, so the history of adultery is in large part the story of individuals who will risk everything of apparent worth for a brief exploration of distant coasts, however paltry.
—Robert Ardrey, *The Territorial Imperative*

Sometimes I wonder if men and women really suit each other. Perhaps they should live next door and just visit now and then.
—Katharine Hepburn

Sex is the most fun you can have without laughing.
—Woody Allen

Masculine expendability proves a part of the cosmic scheme for research and development.
—Howard Bloom, *The Lucifer Principle*

To men, pornos are beautiful love stories with all the boring stuff taken out.
—Richard Jeni

Men and women are a lot alike in certain situations. Like when they're both on fire, they're exactly alike.
—Dave Attell

Men are delusional. Hugh Hefner lounges around in a bathrobe with three live-in girlfriends. You know guys are sitting at home watching the Playboy channel and thinking, "That could be me. I've got a bathrobe."
—Denise Munro Robb

The battle of the sexes is quite a pleasant one.
—Gabriel Laub

Man is sexually compartmentalized. Genitally, he is condemned to a perpetual pattern of linearity, focus, aim, directedness. He must learn to aim. Without aim, urination and ejaculation end in infantile soiling of self or surroundings. Man's genital concentration is a reduction but also an intensification. In sex as in life, they are driven beyond—beyond the self, beyond the body. Even in the womb this rule applies. Every fetus becomes female unless it is steeped in male hormone. Before birth, therefore, a male is already beyond the female. But to be beyond is to be exiled from the center of life. Men know they are sexual exiles. They wander the earth seeking satisfaction, craving and despising, never content. There is nothing in that anguished notion for women to envy.
—Camille Paglia, *Sexual Personae*

Love is the answer, but while you're waiting for the answer, sex raises some pretty good questions.
—Woody Allen

Even in civilized mankind faint traces of monogamous instinct can be perceived.
—Bertrand Russell

The other night I ate at a real nice family restaurant. Every table had an argument going.
—George Carlin

Yeats believed the tragedy of sexual intercourse is that while the fallen world is undone, it comes back again shortly.
—Catherine Cavanaugh, *Love and Forgiveness in Yeats' Poetry*

You know what I like more than women? Pornography. Because I can get pornography.
—Patton Oswalt

My toughest fight was with my first wife.
—Muhammad Ali

I have known more men destroyed by the desire to have wife and child and to keep them in comfort than I have seen destroyed by drink and harlots.
—William Butler Yeats

Sex without love is an empty experience, but as empty experiences go it's one of the best.
—Woody Allen

Sudden religious conversion resembles falling in love in many ways, including its non-rationality.
—Julian Huxley, *New Bottles for New Wine*

Marriage is for women the commonest mode of livelihood, and the total amount of undesired sex endured by women is probably greater in marriage than in prostitution.
—Bertrand Russell

There is no way a beautiful woman can live up to what she looks like for any appreciable length of time.
—Kurt Vonnegut, *Timequake*

Men love oral sex because it combines the two activities that the average guy never gets tired of: 1) Sex. 2) Not moving at all.
—Richard Jeni

Wealth and power are means to women; women are means to eternity.
—Matt Ridley, *The Red Queen*

The difference between love and sex is that sex relieves tension and love causes it.
—Woody Allen

Was the Buddha married? His wife would say, "Are you just going to sit around like that all day?"
—Garry Shandling

I've never known a man who wasn't deeply attached on a very emotional level to his beloved vehicle. Whether it was a piece of junk or a masterpiece made no difference. They rode in their metal boxes and were in control of their lives. I think I know why so many men are afraid to make a commitment to women. It's because we can't be steered.
—Rita Rudner

Men don't settle down. Men surrender.
—Chris Rock

They say married men live longer. It just seems longer.
—Bobby Slayton

The threat to hip is not women but domesticity.
—John Leland, *Hip: The History*

As the kingdom of the animal ascends, so likewise ascends the power of the female. She becomes a sexual specialist...
   If it is the behavior of the female towards a particular male that awakens his full sexual response, then we must conclude that the power of sexual choice rests largely with the female, and that sexual competition is not so much between males for the female of their choice, as between females for the male of theirs. And so the male becomes the sexual attraction, and the female in her response the sexual aggressor.
—Robert Ardrey, *African Genesis*

I got married to complicate my thought process. When you're single, your brain is single-minded. Single guys think three things: "I'd like to go out with her," "I'd like to buy one of those," and "I hope those guys win."
—Jerry Seinfeld

Many people when they fall in love look for a little haven of refuge from the world, where they can be sure of being admired when they are not admirable, and praised when they are not praiseworthy.
—Bertrand Russell

Feminism is going to make it possible for the first time for men to be free.
—Floyd Dell

The Bible may be the Greatest Story Ever Told, but the most popular story you can ever tell is about a good-looking couple having a really swell time copulating outside wedlock, and having to quit for one reason or another while doing it is still a novelty.
—Kurt Vonnegut, *Timequake*

I know what men want. Men want to be really, really close to someone who will leave them alone.
—Elayne Boosler

I first learned the concepts of non-violence in my marriage.
—Mahatma Gandhi

Every single one of my friends from high school has long since tied the knot. And I'm getting older. I guess I should think about hanging myself, too.
—Laura Kightlinger

Of course, women love men who have lots of money, don't they? Oh, come on. They do. If I were a woman I'd love them too. Why do you think men fritter their lives away trying to earn the stuff? Men used to vie for women with fists and clubs and teeth. Now they use money. That sounds like an improvement to me.
—Martin Amis, *Other People*

You're only as old as who you're feeling.
—Groucho Marx

If you want to give up the admiration of thousands of men for the distain of one, go ahead, get married.
—Katharine Hepburn

The fact that women do not typically engage in [promiscuous] activities by no means implies that their sexual drives are somehow less strong than that of men—only that they desire more control over whom they have sex with.
—William Allman, *The Stone Age Present*

A woman marries hoping he will change, and he doesn't. A man marries hoping she won't change, and she does.
—Joey Bishop

In our Western societies, we have become too credulous about romantic love, just as earlier ages were too credulous about religious faith. Both can often be blind, and then both can mislead us.
—Julian Huxley, *New Bottles for New Wine*

It is an infantile superstition of the human spirit that virginity would be thought a virtue and not the barrier that separates ignorance from knowledge.
—Voltaire

Female tragic protagonists are rare. Tragedy is a male paradigm of rise and fall, a graph in which dramatic and sexual climax are in shadowy analogy. Climax is another western invention. Traditional eastern stories are picaresque, horizontal chains of incident.
—Camille Paglia, *Sexual Personae*

No Funny Stuff

THIS AFFECTS ALL OF US, DUDE

Idealism and Morality

Of all the lazy literary devices out there, perhaps the cheapest is taking a big word and breaking it into pieces to show what it really means. Obviously we're big fans of the lazy and the cheap, so here goes:

Aside from all his business achievements, above all the Big Lebowski fancies himself a philanthropist. *Philanthropy* comes from the Greek words *philos,* "loving" and anthropos, "man." In this sense, love doesn't refer to the physical act of love, but rather its broad, unspecific, self-consciously exhibitionistic expression. Basically, a huge uncensored pornographic swingers party for the soul.

Philanthropists are almost always old rich geezers who made a lot of money any way they could, and now want to give some back. There are many reasons why they do this: a) because they can take it off their taxes; b) to save themselves from the fiery pits of an imaginary hell; c) to win the admiration and respect; and possibly, d) because it sometimes feels nice to help the less fortunate.

Of course, when you don't have a lot of cash on hand but you still want to help other people, nobody calls you a philanthropist. The best you can hope for in this case is "activist" or "idealist." Most of these folks try and help others by jumping up and down and yelling a lot in order to get the people with cash to do something about it. Since "money talks" as they say, you've got to scream loudly to be heard if you haven't got any.

Still, lots of wonderful things are done by people who act selflessly to lend a hand to others, whether they do it by writing a check or penning a blog post. Many honorable crusaders have taken great strides in making the world a better place for all, and those people have been the subjects of many a grand narrative.

The Big Lebowski features none of those people. This is a film about phony philanthropists, untrue believers, the righteous indignant, enfeebled activists, and heavyweight soapboxers who stand up for what they believe in when they really should just sit down and shut the fuck up.

Aside from near-mute Donnie, the Dude is just about the only character in the film not pretending to be big-hearted or hollering his personal ideology from the rooftops: The Big Lebowski trumpets the values of hard work and charity; Walter protests every action as a violation of personal freedom, territory, or the law (Mosaic and otherwise); Maude advertises her feminist agenda on her canvases just as she does in day to day discourse; the Nihilists tirelessly assert their lack of a belief in anything to anyone who'll listen; and even pornographer Jackie Treehorn feels compelled to portray himself as a techno-maverick and political advocate. Everyone's got a dubious "answer for everything" tattooed on their forehead, essentially condescending replies to questions no one asked.

In contrast, the childlike, almost bumbling quality of the Dude's outlook on life stands out against all the certainty principles which cloud around him. In Western culture, people are always instructed that they need to believe in something, but no one ever asks "why?" The vast majority of atrocities committed in history have been performed by supposedly good-intentioned people "believing in something" and acting on it for the good of humanity.

It's not that the Dude believes in nothing—he's no nihilist. It's just that he entertains ideas so gingerly. Since he's never angling from any fixed position, he can examine each new conceptual element without trying to chisel it into some concrete pillar of belief. Taoism calls this approach the "state of the uncarved block." In order to see things as they truly are, the idea goes, we've got to be able to "unlearn" all the carvings (ideas) we take for granted.

Of course, if you questioned every single thing at every moment you'd never be able to get out of bed. A truly uncarved block is as dumb as the proverbial post. The Dude's method of finding a tipsy balance between open-mindedness and idiocy is just not to care so much about being right all the time. This is the exact opposite approach of just about everybody else in the film.

Taoism's younger sister, Zen Buddhism has a lot to say on this matter: basically, all "wrong action" comes from placing too much emphasis on the ego—that is, systematically bending reality towards you, to fit what you want it to be, and what you personally want to receive from it. In other words, what most people call "belief."

Now, at face value it seems pretty egocentric for a guy to call himself "The Dude," and to require that others do so too. Yet perhaps his intentions are the same as activist Malcolm Little when he changed his name to Malcolm X in order to recuse himself from the lineage of his slaveholder ancestors. Likewise, by un-christening himself, the Dude may have decided to uncarve his own tree of his life and start all over again.

It's not a new idea. Changing one's name has long been common practice for people entering orders of brotherhood and sisterhood in various religions all over the world, not to mention a career in pop or hip hop music.

As inadvertently philanthropic Dude shows, if you truly love humanity, one good and very underrated way to share that love is to do nothing at all—neither bad nor self-consciously good. This is one of the central objectives of Taoism: to minimize the impact of our existence upon the world.

And it's not just some kind of eastern thing either: Voltaire and Samuel Johnson, the two greatest philosophers of the European Enlightenment period both addressed the nature of progress in books that were published almost simultaneously—*Candide*, and *Rasselas: Prince of Abyssinia*, respectively. After sending their protagonists on long journeys of inquiry, both books concluded that the only way to truly make the world a better place was to "tend to your own little garden."

Don't have a little garden? Then tend to your rug. The idea is, if we tie our rooms together, the whole world will hopefully follow. Most importantly of all, don't micturate on the rugs (or gardens) of your neighbors. The "Golden rule" is still the highest ideal humanity ever came up with. Like gold itself, it remains untarnished and incorruptible. Ever thus to goldbrickers.

Voltaire once famously pointed out that the problem with idealism is that often, "The ideal is the enemy of the good." From which, we Dudeists might happily infer, "The easygoing is the friend of the far out."

An idealist is one who, on noticing that roses smell better than a cabbage, concludes that it will also make better soup.
—H.L. Mencken

Insanity in individuals is something rare—but in groups, parties, nations and epochs, it is the rule.
—Friedrich Nietzsche

Morality is simply the attitude we adopt towards people whom we personally dislike.
—Oscar Wilde

Contempt for happiness is usually contempt for other people's happiness, and is an elegant disguise for hatred of the human race.
—Bertrand Russell

Do what you feel in your heart to be right—for you'll be criticized anyway.
—Eleanor Roosevelt

As far as I'm concerned, I prefer silent vice to ostentatious virtue.
—Albert Einstein

I know a man who gave up smoking, drinking, sex, and rich food. He was healthy right up to the day he killed himself.
—Johnny Carson

What you do speaks so loud that I cannot hear what you say.
—Ralph Waldo Emerson

Equality may perhaps be a right, but no power on earth can ever turn that into a fact.
—Honoré de Balzac

Good friends, good books and a sleepy conscience: this is the ideal life.
—Mark Twain

The most widespread beliefs draw their power from the fact that they cannot be verified.
—Alessandro Morandotti

If you obey all the rules, you miss all the fun.
—Katharine Hepburn

There's a deception to every rule.
—Hal Lee Luyah

Preach the gospel at all times and, if necessary, use words.
—Saint Francis of Assisi

Morality is the custom of one's country and the current feeling of one's peers. Cannibalism is moral in a cannibal country.
—Samuel Butler

What emerges from the tangle is a very funny film about real things and the search for meaning: not just the solution to a mystery, but an ethos by which to navigate a jumbled place in jumbled times.
—J.M. Tyree & Ben Walters, *BFI Film Classics: The Big Lebowski*

Believe those who are seeking the truth. Doubt those who find it.
—Andre Gide

When I was younger I could not focus on anything, or even apprehend a single thought, without feeling driven to incorporate it into some architectonic, some Great Design.
—Will Self, *Grey Area*

The opportunity for doing mischief is found a hundred times a day, and of doing good once in a year.
—Voltaire

Inside every cynical person, there is a disappointed idealist.
—George Carlin

Because the story has been told so often, it has taken root in every man's mind. And, as with all retold tales that are in people's hearts, there are only good and bad things and black and white things and good and evil things and no in-between anywhere.
—John Steinbeck, *The Pearl*

The brotherhood of man is evoked by particular men according to their circumstances. But it seldom extends to all men. In the name of our freedom and our brotherhood we are prepared to blow up the other half of mankind and to be blown up in our turn.
—R. D. Laing

The infliction of cruelty with a good conscience is a delight to moralists. That is why they invented Hell.
—Bertrand Russell

First comes grub, then morality.
—Bertolt Brecht

Ethics is in origin the art of recommending to others the sacrifices required for cooperation with oneself.
—Bertrand Russell

All truths are half-truths.
—Alfred North Whitehead

If we could just get everyone to close their eyes and visualize world peace for an hour, imagine how serene and quiet it would be until the looting started.
—from a 15 year old applicant to a *"Deep Thoughts by Jack Handey"* newspaper contest.

When we start deceiving ourselves into thinking not that we want something or need something, not that it is a pragmatic necessity for us to have it, but that it is a moral imperative that we have it, then is when we join the fashionable madmen, and then is when the thin whine of hysteria is heard in the land, and then is when we are in bad trouble.
—Joan Didion, *Slouching Towards Bethlehem*

I do have a test today. That wasn't bullshit. It's on European socialism. I mean, really, what's the point? I'm not European. I don't plan on being European. So who cares if they're socialists? They could be fascist anarchists. It still doesn't change the fact that I don't own a car. Not that I condone fascism, or any *ism* for that matter. Isms in my opinion are not good. A person should not believe in an ism, he should believe in himself. I quote John Lennon, "I don't believe in The Beatles, I just believe in me." Good point there. After all, he was the walrus. I could be the walrus. I'd still have to bum rides off people.
—Ferris Bueller, *Ferris Bueller's Day Off (1986)*. Screenplay by John Hughes

190 – Idealism and Morality

The greatest tragedy in mankind's entire history may be the hijacking of morality by religion.
—Arthur C. Clarke

You are never dedicated to something you have complete confidence in. No one is fanatically shouting that the sun is going to rise tomorrow. They *know* it's going to rise tomorrow. When people are fanatically dedicated to political or religious faiths or any other kinds of dogmas or goals, it's always because these dogmas or goals are in doubt.
—Robert Pirsig, Zen and the Art of Motorcycle Maintenance

It seems to be the fate of idealists to obtain what they have struggled for in a form which destroys their ideals.
—Bertrand Russell

It has been my experience that folks who have no vices have very few virtues.
—Abraham Lincoln

The trouble with being a responsible citizen is that it takes up too many evenings.
—Todd Buchholz, *From Here to Economy*

Moral indignation is jealousy with a halo.
—H.G. Wells

My conscience, I may tell myself, is my own. It is anything but my own. Nothing I seem to possess is so little my own. It is the exclusive property of those territorial or social institutions of which I am a part.
—Robert Ardrey, *African Genesis*

Cynicism is the imagination of the mediocre.
—Joe Klein

Was there any clean money on earth? Had there ever been any? No. Categorically. Even the money paid to the most passionate nurses, the dreamiest artists, freshly painted, very dry, and shallowly embossed to the fingertips, had its origin in some bastardly on the sweatshop floor.
—Martin Amis, *London Fields*

Beware of the pursuit of the Superhuman: it leads to an indiscriminate contempt for the Human. To a man, horses and dogs and cats are mere species, outside the moral world. Well, to the Superman, men and women are mere species too, also outside the moral world.
—George Bernard Shaw, *Man and Superman*

What realm of human endeavor is not morally ambiguous? Even folk institutions that purport to give us advice on behavior and ethics seem fraught with contradictions. Consider aphorisms: Haste makes waste. Yes, but a stitch in time saves nine. Better safe than sorry; but nothing ventured nothing gained. Where there's smoke, there's fire; but you can't tell a book by its cover. A penny saved is a penny earned; but you can't take it with you. He who hesitates is lost; but fools rush in where angels fear to tread. Two heads are better than one; but too many cooks spoil the broth.
—Carl Sagan, *The Demon-Haunted World*

Fanaticism consists of redoubling your effort when you have forgotten your aim.
—George Santayana

Idealism is based on big ideas. And, as anybody who has ever been asked "What's the big idea?" knows, most big ideas are bad ones.
—P.J. O'Rourke, *All the Trouble in the World*

Bale out your individual boat if you can, but the sea remains the sea.
—Herman Melville, *Ramon*

People watch the fall of the ideal bird as it flies over the vapor of stagnant water and they laugh. It is a useful laughter: for each hero whom it hits, it crushes a hundred frauds.
—José Ortega y Gasset, *Meditations on Quixote*

First, the sage never tries to do good, because this requires having a concept of good, which leads to having a concept of evil, which leads to combating evil, which only makes evil stronger. Second, the Sage never tries to do good, because "every straight is doubled by a crooked, every good by an ill." Human affairs are complex: good done to one person may be evil to another.
—Holmes Welch, *Taoism: The Parting of the Way*

Every major horror of history was committed in the name of an altruistic motive. Has any act of selfishness ever equaled the carnage perpetrated by disciples of altruism?
—Ayn Rand

Don Quixote is a symbol before he is a man and his defeats are the defeats of the principle for which he stands...The significant thing about this novel—its claim to be twice over a tragedy—is that it not only shows us the defeat of the man of noble feelings by the second-rate and vulgar, but that it convinces us that the defeat was right.
—Lowry Nelson, Jr., *Cervantes: A Collection of Critical Essays*

Ramblin' Again

THE PREFERRED NOMENCLATURE

Language and Conversation

If there's one thing that separates human beings from the animals, it's not that we kill members of our own species or invent stuff that makes us miserable. What truly sets us apart from the animals is language. More than anything else, human beings are distinguished by their disinclination to shut the fuck up.

The bulk of our days are spent blathering to each other and when we're not talking, we're reading printed material, communicating via email, et cetera. Even when engaged in the most animalistic behavior of all—humping—many of us feel compelled to "talk dirty." Afterwards, we fall asleep and have dreams in which we continue have nonsensical conversations. To top it off, some of us even talk out loud in our sleep. Even if you don't believe in reincarnation, dying isn't always the end of it as people will still continue to echo or interpret anything you may have once said or written down. In an era in which practically everyone on earth has a blog or a Facebook page, it seems that no conversation will ever definitively come to an end.

Even when we're not talking or reading, we're using words to think. As linguists point out, without language, thinking isn't really possible for us. Children who for whatever reason never learn to speak never really learn to think either, and grow up with hamburger for brains. One suspects that as a youth, Dude and Walter's poor dimwitted partner Donny may have spent many an afternoon locked in the pantry.

There are many things that make the films of the Coen Brothers remarkable, but chief among them is their attention to language. Each of their movies documents a subset of the American cultural landscape, and although judiciously selected clothing and set design play a big part, the orienting device of each film is usually a convincing employment of native vernacular. In other words: the language for its time and place. From the Hicksville argot of *Raising Arizona* to the rapid-fire Manhattan exchanges of *The Hudsucker Proxy* to the laconic Scandinavian-inflected yak of *Fargo*, the Coens have shown how closely intertwined personal identity can be with the parlance of our minds.

Of course, few real people actually talk the way characters do in Coen films—their films portray a selectively enhanced form of authenticity, where everyone speaks a hyper-naturalistic style of conversational poetry in which nary a word is misplaced.

What makes watching a Coen Brothers film such a joy is that no matter how stupid a character may be, he will always put things *just-so*, in a manner tellingly wise in its own way, even if it may initially seem idiotic. It's as if the Coens are humanistically pointing out that everyone has the potential for a rare brand of genius, even though they might not realize it themselves.

The implication here is that a high road transcending the banality of everyday life can be reached via a deliberate and tasteful enhancement of language. Conversely, to settle for ordinary, mediocre discourse is to shrug off what makes us especially human, to carelessly reject an extraordinary evolutionary birthright.

In a day and age when too many American schoolchildren repeatedly use the word "like" to indicate they can't think of an actual word, such a creative appreciation for language would be a great thing to teach in school. Exposed to the psychedelic pleasures of everyday poetry, maybe our Little Lebowskis wouldn't spend so much time smoking Thai stick or driving around, and instead pay attention in class. The Dude wasn't against college, after all; he was only against the dross they were regurgitating and reheating—he even said so himself in the real-life Port Huron Statement.

Indeed it's well known that many people don't "get" *The Big Lebowski* because they find the plot wanting. Yet what makes the film such a treasure is not the story itself, nor even its characters, but the mind-blowing verbal pleasure they afford us.

Take a close look at the screenplay: Virtually every single line in the film could convincingly be printed on a T-shirt. If we all expressed ourselves this way, as if leaving something behind for posterity, it would help raise the art of living to a new level. We are what we speak. To blather gracefully conveys more charisma than stylish sunglasses, nail polish or a pressed suit ever could.

Thus, when the reactionary police chief of Malibu says "let me make something plain" before launching into a typically unimaginative verbal attack on the Dude, he is being far more candid than he realizes. Like other fascists throughout history, the man is both dull and ugly down to his soul, something made perfectly plain by his robot rhetoric.

Bush-league psych-out stuff, man! Ultimately, Chief Kohl only gets through to the Dude by bashing him on the head with a coffee mug. It's no wonder: violence is the epic poetry of the inarticulate.

I remain convinced that obstinate addiction to ordinary language in our private thoughts is one of the main obstacles to progress in philosophy.
—Bertrand Russell

True spirituality consists in making the heart and the lips the same.
—Sri Ramakrishna

Man invented language to satisfy his deep need to complain.
—Lily Tomlin

Only kings, presidents, editors, and people with tapeworms have the right to use the editorial "we."
—Mark Twain

In science one tries to tell people, in such a way as to be understood by everyone, something that no one ever knew before. But in poetry, it's the exact opposite.
—Paul Dirac

A good listener is usually thinking about something else.
—Kin Hubbard

I am so clever that sometimes I don't understand a single word of what I am saying.
—Oscar Wilde

The real meaning of a word is only as powerful or harmless as the emotion behind it.
—Sarah Silverman

The mouth obeys poorly when the heart murmurs.
—Voltaire

"When I use a word," Humpty Dumpty said in a rather scornful tone, "it means just what I choose it to mean—neither more nor less."
    "The question is," said Alice, "whether you *can* make words mean so many different things."
    "The question is," said Humpty Dumpty, "who is to be master—that's all."
—Lewis Carroll, *Through the Looking Glass.*

In another widespread African story, apes *can* talk, but prudently refuse to do so—because talking apes, their intelligence in this way made manifest, will be put to work by humans. Their silence is proof of their intelligence.
—Carl Sagan & Ann Druyan, *Shadows of Forgotten Ancestors*

Quotation is a serviceable substitute for wit.
—Oscar Wilde

The Christian receives his name through the sacred rite of baptism; monks and nuns get their spiritual names when they enter their orders; Lovers all over the world find new pet names for each other.
—Joseph Campbell, introduction to *Mothers and Amazons* by Helen Diner

Is sloppiness in speech caused by ignorance or apathy? I don't know and I don't care.
—William Safire

Comparing our brains anatomically with chimpanzee brains (or dolphin brains or any other non-human brains) would be almost beside the point, because our brains are in effect joined together into a single cognitive system that dwarfs all others. They are joined by an innovation that has invaded our brains and no others: language. I am not making the foolish claim that all our brains are knit together by language into one gigantic mind, thinking its transnational thoughts, but, rather that each individual human brain, thanks to its communicative links, is the beneficiary of the cognitive labors of the others in a way that gives it unprecedented powers.
—Daniel Dennett, *Darwin's Dangerous Idea*

The 20th century linguistic revolution is the recognition that language is not merely a device for communicating ideas about the world, but rather a tool for bringing the world into existence in the first place.
—Misia Landau

To articulate opinion is not to create it. Nor is it to leave it as it was. Men understand their opinions better when they articulate them. They not only frame their opinions into words, they form the opinion by framing it.
—Owen Chadwick, *The Secularization of the European Mind in the 19th Century*

It is no coincidence that terms describing a witty exchange—thrust, parry, riposte, repartee—come from swordplay.
—Camile Paglia, *Sexual Personae*

Forgive me my nonsense as I forgive the nonsense of those who think they talk sense.
—Robert Frost

The great rule: If the little bit you have is nothing special in itself, at least find a way of saying it that is a little bit special.
—George Christoph Lichtenberg

Any lengthy talking among Rastas is known as "reasoning."
—Tracy Nicholas, *Rastafari—A Way of Life*

To understand a name you must be acquainted with the particular of which it is a name.
—Bertrand Russell

The fish trap exists because of the fish; once you've gotten the fish, you can forget the trap. The rabbit snare exists because of the rabbit; once you've gotten the rabbit, you can forget the snare. Words exist because of the meaning; once you've gotten the meaning, you can forget the words. Where can I find a man who has forgotten words so I can have a word with him?
—Chuang Tzu

You Said It

WHAT THE FUCK ARE YOU TALKING ABOUT?

The "F" word

It should come as no surprise even to the casual viewer that *The Big Lebowski* enjoys one of the highest frequencies of the word "fuck" or its variants in the history of cinema—ranking around number 24 in order of "most fucked" with 281 unabashed utterances, averaging one every 25 seconds. As one might expect most of the other entries on the list are crime dramas where people try to kill each other a lot.

What's telling, however, is that if you only count comedies, *The Big Lebowski* comes in at #3. Plus, if you count comedies that are actually funny (#1 and #2 are *Twin Town* and *Made*) then Lebowski easily takes the Academy Award for Most Fucked Film Worldwide. Nothing is fucked here!

The fact that TBL is both so full of "fucks" and also a feel-good comedy is far out indeed. In crime dramas people yell "fuck" because they hate each other, or because they've just had a body part torn off. But when people drop the F-bomb in *The Big Lebowski* they're mostly doing it because it's fucking funny. For some alchemical reason, the word "fuck" enhances a punch line in the way "consequently" enhances an argument. Moreover, the word underscores a central theme of the film: male frustration, both sexual and societal. Yet these are only the most obvious reasons for the fuckload of F words in the film. There may be something deeper to it than that—an element, dare we say, spiritual?

For such a poetically scripted, at times erudite film, the frequency of profanities stands out like a slew of severed toes. The Coens cleverly acknowledge this incongruity, however: At the midway point in the film, the film's cowboy narrator shows up like some Okie Wan Kenobi to offer the Dude helpful counsel on how to overcome his adversaries. And yet his only advice is: "Do you have to use so many cuss words?"

Tendered to a man in whom many would see myriad other failures other than bad language, the Stranger's remark comes off as uniquely perspicacious: The Dude's greatest flaw may very well be his overuse of the term "fuck," though not because it's impolite or uncouth, but because it's so plainly unimaginative. The Dude, after all, is an unwitting master of idiom, creatively and effortlessly refashioning snippets of canny lingo from everyone around him. Surely he could do better than merely aping his macho contemporaries by falling back far too often on an overused expletive—a word which is, like Shakespeare's definition of life itself, "full of sound and fury, signifying nothing."

Then again, words which signify nothing can often be profoundly mystical in their unmeaning. "Life," for instance is a perfect example. What's the meaning of "life"? It's an old question, and neither its definition nor its purpose has been convincingly settled. Or even better: "God." Not only do people use "God" in just about as many different ways as they do "fuck" and its variants—plea, interjection, curse, adjective, et cetera, but no one can agree on what the word is meant to represent in the first place.

Yet that's why words like these exist: to try to *eff* the ineffable. However ineffective as they may ultimately be, they act as proverbial Zen fingers pointing at (and in some cases, flipping off) the moon.

The Big Lebowski is so full of the word "fuck" and its variants that one almost suspects it was written that way on purpose. Given the deeply philosophical nature of the film it's possible that "fuck" is a sort of mantra of suffering, repeated by hard-pressed creatures barking reflexively at shadows.

To prevent him from entering a world of pain, the Stranger offers the Dude this simple, helpful suggestion, like a Zen master providing a koan to a student on the brink of Buddhahood. Ultimately, the Dude does decide to truly enlighten up, and by story's end, his mannered mentor takes comfort in that. To wit: their final meeting is utterly fuck-free.

It should also be noted here that there are two other important words in the film that share nearly as much screen time (as well as mystical ambiguity) as the word "fuck": "Dude," which is spoken 161 times, and "man," 147 times.

With all these vague filler words floating around it's a wonder the Coens found space for such precise gems as "compeer," "micturate," and "nomenclature." This just goes to prove that regardless of any other lists it might feature on, *The Big Lebowski* is certainly unparalleled in cinematic history when it comes to joining the highbrow with the low.

Joo said it, mang. Laughable!

Just as gunpowder was invented around the time of the word fuck, so now we have long range missiles. The age of the mass fuck is upon us...

Soldiers are intimately connected with fuck, and that's why they're addicted to the word. They get it from all sides.
—Wing F. Fing, *Fuck Yes!*

Born of fucking, dead from fucking, living fucked: pregnant belly and winding sheet, hidden in the word...the fraternity of the fucked. Chain gang of the fucked, linked before and behind, joined to all who have lost and preceded us, to all who will lose and follow us: heir to being fucked by those who stand above you: child of the children of the word, father of sons of the word.
—Carlos Fuentes, *The Death of Artemio Cruz*

The most potent form of verbal abuse in English and many other languages is "Fuck you," with the pronoun "I" implicit at the beginning. The speaker is vividly asserting his claim to higher status, and his contempt for those he considers subordinate. Characteristically, humans have converted a postural image into a linguistic one with barely a nuance. The phrase is uttered millions of times each day, all over the planet, with hardly anyone stopping to think what it means. Often, it escapes our lips unbidden. It is satisfying to think what it means. Often, it escapes our lips unbidden. It is satisfying to say. It serves its purpose. It is a badge of the primate order, revealing something of our nature despite all our denials and pretensions.
—Carl Sagan & Ann Druyan, *Shadows of Forgotten Ancestors*

One reason *fuck* may be used so often is that immigrants didn't understand why the slang for making love was dirtier than the slang for going to the bathroom.
—P.J. O'Rourke, *Eat the Rich*

Fuck is like Belgium. People fight over it. It doesn't really have anything to do with Belgium or with fuck. People need to fight over certain things that Belgium and fuck happen to be in the way of.
—Dave Marsh, *Fuck (A Documentary) (2005)*

Money doesn't talk, it swears.
—Bob Dylan

It's a rather rude gesture, but at least it's clear what you mean.
—Katharine Hepburn

We shouldn't curse with sexual words. It gives sex a bad name, and it doesn't make sense. You're driving, someone cuts you off on the road, almost kills you, you roll down the window, wish them the nicest possible thing in the world. We need new curses that really mean something, like, "Oh, yeah? Audit you, buddy."
—Elayne Boosler

Let us swear while we may, for in heaven it will not be allowed.
—Mark Twain

The only difference between graffiti and philosophy is the word "fuck."
—Anonymous

The term man for instance as in "hey man," a phrase used a few million times by me and my old partner Cheech, was a reaction in the forties and fifties by the black jazz musicians to the derogatory term boy, which was used by white racists when they addressed black men.
—Tommy Chong, from the introduction to *Pot Culture* by Shirley Halperin and Steve Bloom

What-Have-You

THERE'S NOT A LITERAL CONNECTION

Art, Literature & Film

For the last goddamn time, what's *The Big Lebowski* all about?

Like any great piece of art, it really depends on who you ask. We've endeavored to cover a great variety of viewpoints in this book—lotta strands in old Dudeism's head. As Dude says, "It's not just, it might not be, just such a simple, uh—you know?" So what's it all about? Well, Dude, we just don't know…

It's about what makes a man.

It's a commentary on war and activism.

It's stock-taking in the aftermath of the 1960s.

It's about how friendship and self-respect is more important than status.

It's about the emasculation of the modern American male.

It's about America itself.

It's a lesson on how not to get worked up over a whole bunch of nothing.

It's a Western reworking of eastern philosophy.

It's a neo-noir genre-buster.

It's a silly buddy/stoner comedy with no point whatsoever.

It's just a game, man.

It's a fucking travesty.

It's just, like, uh, your opinion.

It's, uh…lost my train of thought there.

Making sense of *The Big Lebowski* is a bit like making sense of the Mona Lisa or *Moby Dick*. Nobody knows for sure what Da Vinci or Melville had in mind when they helped them to be conceived. But of course, it doesn't matter: Good art increases the chances of its own conception. The genius of others grabs our own genius and beats it out of us. Peering at itself through that Time/Life mirror, the universe recognizes its own best interests almost as if by accident.

It's easy to overlook, but *The Big Lebowski* is actually chock full of artists. Maude is the most obvious, of course, with her highly-commended "vaginal" paintings. But also: Marty, the interpretive dancer; Arthur Digby Sellers, the successful TV writer; Autobahn, the 80s techno band the Nihilists once helmed; Knox Harrington, the sniggering video artist; Bunny, the aspiring erotica ingénue; even the Dude himself had a minor musical career in Metallica (as a roadie), not to mention the fact that he also penned uncompromised political manifestos in his college years. Hell, even sleazy porn filmmaker Jackie Treehorn fancies himself a serious auteur at odds with the amateurs in his industry—plus, he's a pretty gifted sketch artist too.

Of course, this is all part and parcel of a film set in a town like Los Angeles—where every waiter is an actor, and every cashier a screenwriter. But the notion of reinvention that is so central to the Los Angeles landscape is also the cornerstone of art.

Aside from all the other things *The Big Lebowski* may be, it is also a commentary on the pitfalls of artistic identity—what it means to be truly independent and trailblazing in a civilization expressly designed to homogenize the human personality. Sadly, like many self-styled "artists," the outwardly artistic characters generally pursue this freedom for the purpose of self-aggrandizement. The only artist who seems humble at all (he asks for "notes") is Marty. It's too bad he's so endearingly awful.

Where does the Dude stand as an artist? As a dilettante of the highest degree, it is only he who can realize the purest art of all: The Art of Living. Thus the Dude is a Da Vinci of the Day-to-day, a Michelangelo of the mundane, a savant of the subtle. His *modus operandi* is his *magnum opus*.

This is why The Stranger refers to him in the same way that others who stand out among their contemporaries have been referred to: As "the man for his time and place."

Why? Because the Dude is a man who's taken the promise of liberty and freedom and emerged at the edge of civilization to instruct us exactly how to use it: Not to make ourselves glamorous in the eyes of others; not to right all the wrongs in the world; not to oppress the less-powerful; not to preach big messages, but to remind us all that freedom—personal, individual freedom—is an overarching and all-important end-in-itself. Unlike Tolkien's fantasy epics, it is not a ring that will unite us, but a ringer: The promise of emptiness and unloading.

Freedom is what art has striven towards since its inception—an unfettered avenue upon which we can break the heavy bonds of nature and physics and more aptly enter the realms of the imagination. And of course it's a process, not a place. To focus too much on the product of our art is merely to concentrate on its meat, not its method. At the end of the day, the products of art are only dildoed doodles on our own signature stationery. They are signposts on the road to Death Valley which help keep us from having to double back or lose our train of thought.

Like the Taoist "uncarved block," the Dude reminds us that we ourselves are the canvas upon which we paint our personalities. In life as in art, we don't usually understand much of what we're looking at because it's all up to interpretation. And so we paint a bit, and then we step back and ponder. And then we paint over it and ponder again.

In expertly reminding us of this, he fixes the cable—down through the ages, across the neural strands of time. The billboards will burn, but the road remains. Westward the wagons. It is upon this infinitely unfolding frontier that the Dude abides, simultaneously still life and landscape.

It's no wonder that truth is stranger than fiction. Fiction has to make sense.
—Mark Twain

Isaac Asimov, who is a great man, perceives three stages so far in the development of American Science fiction, says we are in stage three now.
    1) Adventure dominant
    2) Technology dominant
    3) Sociology dominant
    I can hope that this is a prophetic outline of Earthling history too.
—Kurt Vonnegut, *Wampeters, Foma and Granfalloons*

My role in society, or any artist's or poet's role, is to try and express what we all feel. Not to tell people how to feel. Not as a preacher, not as a leader, but as a reflection of us all.
—John Lennon

Long periods of languor, indolence and staring at the ceiling are needed by any creative person in order to develop ideas.
—Tom Hodgkinson, *How to be Idle*

So now I believe that the only way in which Americans can rise above their ordinariness, can mature sufficiently to rescue themselves and to help rescue their planet, is through enthusiastic intimacy with works of their own imaginations.
—Kurt Vonnegut, *Wampeters, Foma and Granfalloons*

Artists historically play pivotal roles in fomenting cultural and political revolutions. It now seems that they may have always played such a role and that art was at the center of the revolution from which fully modern humans emerged...
    How paradoxical that the most striking archeological signature of the full-blown emergence of our own human species turns out to be not new and better hand axes but symbolic art. It is precisely nonutilitarian art that bears the greatest significance in showing that modern humans had made the leap to assigning value to objects that went beyond practical day-to-day needs. Symbolic and spiritual thinking are in many respects the same process.
—Donald Johanson, *Ancestors*

In every work of genius we recognize our own rejected thoughts; they come back to us with a certain alienated majesty.
—Ralph Waldo Emerson

You want to know how to paint a perfect painting? It's easy. Make yourself perfect and just paint naturally.
—Robert Pirsig, *Zen and the Art of Motorcycle Maintenance*

The Big Lebowski might be a thing of rags and patches, then, but it's not simply an extended exercise in hollow pastiche; rather it's a film *about* pastiche, about sampling, magpieism, the putting on of identities, the patchwork nature of Los Angeles—and about the movies themselves.
—J.M. Tyree & Ben Walters, *BFI Film Classics: The Big Lebowski*

Just let the wardrobe do the acting.
—Jack Nicholson

Modern art is what happens when painters stop looking at girls and persuade themselves that they have a better idea.
—John Ciardi

Every child is an artist. The problem is how to remain an artist once he grows up.
—Pablo Picasso

The moment you think you understand a great work of art, it's dead for you.
—Oscar Wilde

What artists have accomplished is realizing that there's only a small amount of stuff that's important, and then seeing what it was.
—James Gleick, *Chaos*

…our own ever-growing predicament: there is nothing so boring in life, let alone in cinema, as the boredom of being excited all the time.
—Anthony Lane

Casablanca became a cult movie because it is not one movie. It is "movies." And this is the reason it works, in defiance of any aesthetic theory.
—Umberto Eco, *Travels in Hyperreality*

What you need is something people are in denial about that they want to see you take the risk of expressing.
—George W. S. Trow, *Within the Context of No Context*

The point I discovered is that the best technique is none at all. I never feel that I must adhere to any particular manner of approach. I try to remain open and flexible, ready to turn with the wind or with the current of thought. That's my stance, my technique, if you will, to be flexible and alert, to use whatever I think good at the moment.
—Henry Miller

The sidekick of twentieth-century American popular culture seems made of different stuff. In contrast with the hero, who has typically been an intrepid, honest, somewhat humorless, and often not overbright white male, the sidekick has typically been a person socially stigmatized in one way or another, whether by being black, Native American, foreign, a child, a woman, an oaf, or physically handicapped. Thus Batman's tireless fight against crime was assisted by the Boy Wonder, Robin, the Lone Ranger had his faithful Indian companion, Tonto (whose name in Spanish means "stupid"); and the Cisco Kid roamed the West accompanied by the overweight buffoon Pancho. The hero often has a double identity as well—one as hero, frequently masked or otherwise outlandishly costumed, and the other as ordinary Joe, the hero's presentation of self in everyday life.

Interpretations of the true meaning of the hero-sidekick relationship abound. Is it significant that both Cisco and Pancho are diminutives for the same name (Francisco)? Again, the physical subtext may be the splitting of a single protagonist into the heroic (essentially tragic) and loutish (hence comical) components in us all; while we would all like to be capable of heroism, we really identify with the flawed, fallible buddy.
—Alexander Humez, Nicholas Humez and Joseph Maguire, *Zero to Lazy Eight*

Our fundamental tactic of self-protection, self-control, and self-definition is not spinning webs or building dams, but telling stories, and more particularly concocting and controlling the story we tell others—and ourselves—about who we are. We do not consciously and deliberately figure out what narratives to tell and how to tell them. Our tales are spun, but for the most part we don't spin them; they spin us. Our human consciousness, and our narrative selfhood, is their product, not their source.
—Daniel Dennett, *Consciousness Explained*

There have been cultures without counting, cultures without painting, cultures bereft of the wheel or the written word, but never a culture without music.
—John Barrow, *The Artful Universe*

It is not as though the so-called surrealists, impressionists, expressionists and neo-romantics were concealing a grand secret by pretending folly; they are concealing their unhappy lack of a secret.
—Robert Graves, *The White Goddess*

Pictures are famous for their humanness, and not for their pictureness.
—Kurt Vonnegut, *Timequake*

Emerson's prophecy of the poet as liberator was fulfilled by Whitman...In its freewheeling structure and perpetual metamorphoses, *Leaves of Grass* is literature's most perfectly Dionysian poetry.
—Camile Paglia, *Sexual Personae*

The search for the historical ancestor of man is the search for the story-teller and the artist.
—Fritjof Capra, *The Web of Life*

The comparison [between movie theaters and temples] is not essentially sacrilegious.
—Lewis Mumford, *The Story of Utopias*

Stanislavsky says there are two kinds of plays. There are plays that you leave, and you say to yourself, "By God, I just, I never, gosh, I want to, *now* I understand! *What* a masterpiece! Let's go get a cup of coffee," and by the time you get home, you can't remember the name of the play, you can't remember what the play was about.

And there are plays—and books and songs and poems and dances—that are perhaps upsetting or intricate or unusual, that you leave unsure, but which you think about perhaps the next day, and perhaps for a week, and perhaps for the rest of your life.

Because they aren't clean, they aren't neat, but there's something in them that comes from the heart, and, so, goes to the heart.
—David Mamet, *Three Uses of the Knife*

Fiction reveals truth that reality obscures.
—Ralph Waldo Emerson

The greater part of the creative dreaming and planning which constitutes literature and art has had very little bearing upon the community in which we live, and has done little to equip us with patterns, with images and ideals, by means of which we might react creatively upon our environment. Yet it should be obvious that if the inspiration for the good life is to come from anywhere, it must come from no other people than the great artists.
—Lewis Mumford, *The Story of Utopias*

People love to be told everything stinks. It sounds so intelligent.
—John Gardner, *On Writers and Writing*

The avant-garde is to the left what jingoism is to the right. Both are a refuge in nonsense. The warm glow of fashion on the left and patriotism on the right evidence individuals' power to elect themselves members of a group superior to reason.
—David Mamet, *Three Uses of the Knife*

Were art to redeem man, it could do so only by saving him from the seriousness of life and restoring him to an unexpected boyishness.
—Jose Ortega y Gasset, *The Dehumanization of Art*

Though hip is a romantic ideal, hip without finance is unpersuasive. Movements in American that don't turn a profit tend to have short lives.
—John Leland, *Hip: The History*

The issue of power and love, knowledge and sympathy, contrivance and imagination, is art; and the highest product of art is not a painting, a statue, a book, a pyramid, but a human personality.
—Lewis Mumford, *Herman Melville*

Aitz Chaim Ha!

THE WHOLE DURNED HUMAN COMEDY

Funny Stuff

Everyone knows that when you try to explain a joke, you extinguish it—it simply ceases to be funny anymore. In the same way that it's impossible to tickle yourself, there must be an element of surprise in all humor. Yet if this is true, how come so many people can watch *The Big Lebowski* over and over again, repeat it's funniest lines, dissect every scene, and still find it hilarious?

We contend this is because the kind of humor in *The Big Lebowski* plumbs depths more profound and breadths more far-reaching than those found in typical comedies. Despite running a standard 117 minutes, it is in fact one of the few comedies in recent history which might be labeled "epic."

Though theories of the comic abound, most of them agree that laughing serves as a way to discharge the stress and anxiety of the human condition; which is why, at extremes, laughter is indistinguishable from weeping. Yet a typical comic work only addresses a small portion of what's hard about being human—nascent sexuality (*American Pie*), pointless violence (*The Three Stooges*), existential horror (*Brazil*), or social anxiety (nearly every British comedy ever made), just to name just a few.

With a big-hearted and humanist bear hug, *The Big Lebowski* takes in all of the four themes above, and of course several more could be ferreted (or marmoted) out as well. Indeed, *The Big Lebowski* offers an empathetically God's-eye view of the world: the totality of the absurd human condition, steadily illuminated in scene after scene.

Moreover, whereas most comedies are disparaging to their characters in order to make us feel better about our lives, we truly laugh *with* the Dude, not *at* him. Few comic protagonists have won such enthusiastic allegiance—we don't just sympathize with the Dude, we care about him as if he were a best friend. Instead of looking down upon him, we exalt and forgive him and his foibles; and as he is a profoundly ordinary fellow, we ourselves are lifted up along with him, and likewise redeemed. Two thousand years ago, Christians attempted the same thing with their own countercultural hero. They enjoyed similar success.

It wasn't long, though, before the Church removed all the humor and horizontalness from Christianity. Comedy's overall effect is to deflate, and to dominate the world's population you need to be pumped full of hot air, looking down on everything from a great height. *The Big Lebowski* never seems to get old or unfunny because serious as it may be at certain times and on certain levels, it portrays life as a giant whoopee cushion. It lets off our steam, as well as the puffed-uppery of those who would seek to elevate themselves unfairly.

The Dude and the Don
Whereas there have been innumerable profound tragedies over the ages, comedies of stature have been relatively few and far between. As far as more recent works go, *Tristram Shandy* by Laurence Sterne, *A Confederacy of Dunces* by John Kennedy Toole and *Catch 22* by Joseph Heller spring immediately to mind. Peer back further and there's Moliere's *Tartuffe*, Voltaire's *Candide*, and Shakespare's *Much Ado About Nothing* to consider. But literary critics pressed to find a true compeer of *Lebowski* might be forced to travel all the way back to the middle ages, to the very birth of the modern novel. Arguably not since Miguel de Cervantes' iconic *Don Quixote de la Mancha* has a story imbued the screwball with such pathos and laced it with such an indelible philosophy.

For those who haven't read it, *Don Quixote* concerns an aging Spanish nobleman who loses his mind and suddenly imagines himself a chivalrous hero. Venturing forth on a fleabag horse into the arid landscape of La Mancha, he tries to right wrongs wherever he goes—only he usually ends up making things worse, largely because he is blinded by romantic idealism. The most well-known scene in the book is the one where he takes a group of windmills to be fearsome giants and unsuccessfully tries to attack their huge, spinning arms.

At its base, *Don Quixote de la Mancha* is a sly refutation of the very principles of faith. This prefigures the humanist revolution in thought which would slowly begin to emerge over the subsequent centuries, one which exalted rationality and personal freedom over fatalism and traditionalism.

Setting
Looking back, it's remarkable how much creative and historical DNA *The Big Lebowski* shares with *El Ingenioso Hidalgo Don Quixote de la Mancha*. In many ways, theirs is the same tale. What's more, the two stories serve as bookends of the European "age of discovery"—beginning with Christopher Columbus and ending in contemporary California. Almost exactly 500 years of beautiful (and not-so-beautiful) tradition. 1492 to 1991.

Cervantes' book was a tombstone of sorts, and a cradle—it marked the end of the middle ages and the beginning of the Spanish Golden Age. It is a novel unique for its time in that it looks simultaneously backwards and forwards, and unlike other milestone works that preceded it (The Odyssey, The Bible, The Divine Comedy), it presaged the concept of progress—instead of pursuing an Eden which had already been, it looked towards a golden age which might yet still be. It was an extraordinarily prescient notion, for Spain, with the rest of Europe on its gilded heels, would shortly enter its most fertile intellectual period since the Ancient Greeks.

Yet ironically, the main character of Quixote, in his disgust at the "idle" elite of this time, sallies forth on his horse with the intention of resurrecting the romance and chivalry of the dying middle ages. Due to his adherence to an outmoded code of ethics, he fails in virtually every one of his objectives. *Quixotic* long ago entered the English lexicon, describing any foolishly idealistic endeavor which ends badly.

The Big Lebowski begins with a quixotic adventure of its own—the United States' ill-conceived invasion of Iraq in the early 1990s. Particularly with the benefit of 21st century hindsight George H.W. Bush's assuming the role of heroic liberator comes off as patently ridiculous. Just as Quixote's clumsy endeavors were designed to bring back an imagined moral perfection to the world, so did a quixotic neoconservative U.S. foreign policy send knights in shining Kevlar to the desert to fight against imaginary weapon mills of mass destruction.

The Dude's subsequent adventure can be seen as a comic illumination on a microscale of this specifically Yankee approach to high-plains heroism. And this is perhaps why the quizzically-cowboyish Stranger character who frames the film comes off so melancholy—it's almost as if he's apologizing for something.

Moreover, like Cervantes in 1605, we too appear to be poised at the end of one era and the beginning of a new one. The centuries-old hegemony of the West in general and America in particular is now beset by a bunch of fucking amateurs. Some kind of Middle Eastern thing? Or is China, man, the issue? Our aggression, hawkish patriots might lament, might soon no longer stand. Could our revolution be over? Is everything fucked here? Or is that just the stress talking?

Character

In his own medieval brand of hawkish patriotism, the character of Quixote is in many ways opposed to the emerging modernism of his time: he is resolutely idealistic and thus irrational, a staunch moral conservative, and fiercely patriotic.

In other words, he is not the Dude. He is more like an early analog of Walter Sobchak. In a remarkable article in Slate Magazine, David Haglund argued that the Dude's best buddy Walter was the harbinger of the coming neoconservative revolution in the United States. How disturbing, then, to make the conceptual leap from Walter to Quixote and be forced to conclude that attitudes have changed so little between the middle ages, the Middle East (Cervantes fought the Turks), and middle America (the neoconservative voter base), half a millennium later?

Of course, had Quixote traveled alone, his story would have become tiresomely repetitive, yet luckily for the "idle reader" (as Cervantes happily addresses his Dudeish audience), the Don is provided with affable sidekick Sancho Panza to sweeten the story and provide a corrective to the erroneous knight errant.

In scene after scene, despite Quixote's grandiose pretensions and book-smarts, it is affable, unpretentious Sancho who clearly proves the wiser and more perspicacious of the two. And despite the fact that he is commonly seen as a bit dimwitted, Lowry Nelson argues:

> [Sancho's] language is more like the authentic speech of a true Vermonter or Irishman than that of the crudely and condescendingly presented provincial stereotypes of fiction; our amusement is sustained by novelty and inventiveness rather than by smug or contemptuous superiority.

Hey, we know that guy! Is little Sancho Panza an ancient Iberian harbinger of our own beloved Dude?

Despite his deeply casual appearance, bumbling behavior and difficulty articulating his thoughts, he is in fact disarmingly clever—certainly more so than his blowhard partner as well as other socially-superior characters peppered throughout. In his practical, unassuming, and clear-eyed approach, he provides a good model for the humanist revolution looming on the horizon. Nevertheless, despite his perspicacity, Sancho's flexible and unworried nature allows him to get caught up in his friend Quixote's delusional schemes.

Just as the Dude and Walter are polar opposites, equally are Quixote and Sancho; yet one of the great joys of the story is that the characters often take on qualities of the other over the course of their adventures. For instance, Sancho becomes repeatedly seduced by riches and power promised by Quixote and other more-dominating figures; meanwhile, the Don softens his views and starts to see the world through Sancho's eyes. Some have suggested that this may have been the first time such a thing happened in fiction—literary characters had previously been as steadfast in their temperament as religious icons.

Just as with Cervantes' duo, we often see the edge between Dude and Walter bleed together: The Dude loses his cool and gets tempted by cash, while Walter turns out not only to prove calmer at times than the Dude, but also more perceptive than we initially presume, and more caring as well. Indeed, the Yin-Yang of Quixote and Sancho seems to rotate at the same oddball angles as that of the Dude and Walter. Like two mirrors, one helps illuminate the persona of the other. This very idea, that character is something fluid, which can be developed or molded, ran counter to most medieval belief and helped set the stage for a more robust and forgiving understanding of the human condition. And that's cool. That's cool.

Theme

Keeping all this in mind, *The Big Lebowski* now appears to be a special inversion of *Don Quixote*. With Sancho Panza now installed as the rightful *hee-ro* of the piece, the tale takes on a delightfully different emphasis. It's still at base a critical parody of heroism, but one which now offers a suitable alternative: Dudeism. That is, to *abide* can be nobler and more heroic than to act.

The proof is in the plotting: At virtually no point in the 800-page novel does The Don come close to achieving anything, despite all his bluster and brouhaha. Indeed, on his deathbed at the end of the book Quixote finally comes to his senses and concedes that all his struggles were for naught. This, of course, would be an unusually tragic ending for a comedy were it not for the fact that he is surrounded by friends who have come to love him despite his insanity, and express grave sorrow at his passing.

There is a principle in professional sitcom writing that there are really only two possible plots: "I just gotta be me" and "Everything will be all right as long as we're together." *Lebowski* and *Quixote* are each an elegant hybrid of both archetypal tales.

It shouldn't come as a surprise that sophisticated comedic works aren't fundamentally different from the average sitcom: Mythologist Joseph Campbell pointed out that since our very beginnings, both the human story and the story we tell about humans has been one in which people test the limits of their environment, only to be picked back by our friends when that limit is finally collided with. Comedy becomes tragedy when either a) we travel too far past those limits or b) our friends are unwilling or unable to pick us up.

The choice is ours: confronted with problems, we can be foolhardy and bullheaded like Quixote and Walter, or cool and limber like Sancho and the Dude. Both strategies can be funny—until, as the saying goes, someone loses an eye. Or, as with poor Donny, an *I*. Except for the occasional rare high-concept comedy like "Weekend at Bernie's," death kills comedy.

If, as we indicated, humor is commonly seen as a means to safely discharge excess anxiety, how much better if it teaches us how to forestall our anxieties in the first place? Sancho and the Dude are among the most brilliant characters in comic literature because they do just that, giving new meaning to the word "comedic hero," as they quite literally rescue us—not from windmills or weapons of mass destruction—but from ourselves.

Conclusion

Just as *Don Quixote* was a milestone which marked the beginning of a promising new era in personal freedom and enlightened thinking, we'd like to imagine that *The Big Lebowski* portends a cultural awakening of our own.

The Big Lebowski's implied "Take it Easy Manifesto" thus stands as the final chapter in the European age of empire: From 1492 onward, the mantle of world hegemony passed from Spain, then to England, and finally to the United States. European culture has had a lot to show for that half-millennia on top, as well as many sins to atone for. The Bush dynasty's attempt to conquer the Middle East looks like it may be the last of its kind, an unfortunate final gambit to file among the quixotic events of history. How ironic it is to note that this 500-year western domination of the planet began immediately after the Muslims were defeated and cast out of Southern Spain? Again: nothing changes.

In any case, once the age of heroes is over, perhaps we can finally try again to realize the dream of civilization which began long before Cervantes' time: how to get to the point where we can just take 'er easy. Could it be time to sally forth for the last and most far-out frontier of them all? That ancient abiding abode where laughter and music and forgiveness and inspired screenplays come from? It's out there somewhere. Let's take another look.

It's your roll, Dude. Mark it lazy eight (∞).

"Will it perhaps be said of us one day that we too, steering westwards, hoped to reach an India—but that it was our fate to be shipwrecked against infinity?" —Friedrich Nietzsche

Bonus additional Lebowski/Quixote connections:

- Both Walter and the Dude wear a variety of goatee—a style of beard made popular in the 17th century, with which Quixote and Sancho tend to also be portrayed.
- Jackie Treehorn's "beach party" begins conspicuously with the image of a happy naked woman being tossed in the air from a circular blanket held by several men. This occurred to Sancho multiple times in *Quixote*, but as a form of punishment.
- Before he changed his name to Don Quixote, the character's name was variously Alonso Quejana—or Quijada, or Quixano or Quesada—all of which sound conspicuously close to "Quintana," which is The Jesus' last name. In fact, The Jesus resembles the slender Quixote far more than Walter, does he not?
- In the introduction, Cervantes admits that his goal was to "produce the downfall and destruction of that mischievous mass of absurdities in the romances of chivalry which, though despised by some, were admired by many." *The Big Lebowski* does a similar service by discrediting the cartoonish heroism inherent in much contemporary cinema.
- Cervantes was the first writer to introduce an omniscient narrator who surprisingly shows up in the story as a real person. To the chagrin of many a traditionally-minded critic of *The Big Lebowski*, the character of The Stranger performs the same otherworldly function.
- Just as the Dude is seduced by the promise of riches, only to discover that it was all a trick engineered by *The Big Lebowski* (there never was any money), so is Sancho Panza seduced by the promise of ruling over his own island, one which doesn't actually exist: It's all part of an elaborate practical joke by two phony "dukes." At the end of it, Sancho concludes that ambition is not worth the trouble it brings him and happily returns to his unfettered life, and his loyal, lunatic friend Quixote.

In the split second where you understand a joke you experience a moment of "enlightenment." This cannot be achieved by "explaining" the joke, *i.e.* by intellectual analysis. This must be well known to enlightened men and women, since they almost invariably show a great sense of humor. In the Tao Te Ching we read, "If it were not laughed at it would not be sufficient for the Tao."
—Fritjov Capra, *The Tao of Physics*

We must accept our pain, change what we can, and laugh at the rest.
—Camille Paglia, *Sexual Personae*

This I conceive to be the chemical function of humor: to change the character of our thought.
—Lin Yutang, *The Importance of Living*

I always want to laugh at the sad stuff. You don't need to laugh at the other stuff.
—Sarah Silverman

The only way to get a belly laugh, I've found is to undermine a surface joke with more unhappiness than most mortals can bear.
—Kurt Vonnegut, *Wampeters, Foma and Granfalloons*

The intelligent man finds almost everything ridiculous, the sensible man hardly anything.
—Johann Wolfgang von Goethe

Since everything is an apparition, perfect in just being what it is, as it is. Having nothing to do with good or bad, acceptance or rejection, you might as well burst out laughing!
—Longchenpa

The aim of a joke is not to degrade the human being but to remind him that he is already degraded.
—George Orwell

Laughter is simply the sudden perception of incongruity between our ideals and the actualities before us.
—Arthur Schopenhauer

Laughter is the shortest distance between two people.
—Victor Borge

Laugh and the world laughs with you. Weep and it keeps on laughing.
—Frank McKinney Hubbard

Irony is the only way I can take myself seriously.
—Ludwig Börne

You don't stop laughing because you grow old; you grow old because you stop laughing.
—Michael Pritchard

Fools laugh at others. Wisdom laughs at itself.
—Osho

If we couldn't laugh, we would all go insane.
—Jimmy Buffett

Common sense and a sense of humor are the same thing, moving at different speeds. A sense of humor is just common sense, dancing.
—William James

The first of April is the day we remember what we are the other 364 days of the year.
—Mark Twain

You may estimate your capacity for comic perception by being able to detect the ridicule of them you love, without loving them less.
—George Meredith, *Essay on Comedy*

The tragic writer takes this world seriously and interprets it; the comic writer creates a new world, a world where bad people are harmless, where stupid people are merry, where Fate is transformed into a Puck-like Chance strongly biased in favor of those who have a sense of humor and a proper appreciation of cakes and ale. The fool is an emancipator.
—Enid Welsford

The comic and tragic views of life no longer exclude each other. Perhaps the most important discovery in modern criticism is the perception that comedy and tragedy are somehow akin, or that comedy can tell us many things about our situation even tragedy cannot.
—Wylie Sypher, *Our New Sense of the Comic*

All great deeds and all great thoughts have a ridiculous beginning.
—Albert Camus

You are always somebody's fool. You get a head start being the first to laugh at yourself.
—Claude Roy

We should consider every day lost on which we have not danced at least once. And we should call every truth false which was not accompanied by at least one laugh.
—Friedrich Nietzsche

Laughter is the result of an expectation which, of a sudden, ends in nothing.
—Immanuel Kant

It might be said that the specific remedy for vanity is laughter, and that the one failing that is essentially laughable is vanity.
—Henri Bergsson, *Laughter*

[Don Quixote's delusion] is a special inversion of common sense. It consists in seeking to mold things on an idea of one's own, instead of molding one's ideas on things.
—Henri Bergsson, *Laughter*

Wit is educated insolence.
—Aristotle

Life is a tragedy for those who feel and a comedy for those who think.
—Jean de la Bruyère

I should only believe in a God that would know how to dance.
—Friedrich Nietzsche, *Thus Spake Zarathustra*

Laughter is above all, a corrective. By laughter, society avenges itself for the liberties taken with it.
—Henri Bergsson, *Laughter*

God is a comedian playing to an audience too afraid to laugh.
—Voltaire

If you're not allowed to laugh in heaven, I don't want to go there.
—Martin Luther

The comic character no longer tries to ceaselessly adapt himself to society.
—Henri Bergsson, *Laughter*

How do jokes work? The beginning of each good one challenges you to think. We are such earnest animals. You try to think of a sensible answer. Why does a chicken cross the road?
    The second part of the joke announces that nobody wants you to think, nobody wants to hear your wonderful answer. You are so relieved to at last meet somebody who doesn't demand that you be intelligent. You laugh for joy.
—Kurt Vonnegut, *Palm Sunday*

He who laughs, lasts.
—Mary Pettibone Poole

Existence is comic inherently. This world is contingency and absurdity incarnate, the oddest of possibilities masquerading momentarily as fact.
—George Santayana

Seriousness is an accident of time. It consists in putting too high a value on time. In eternity there is no time. Eternity is a mere moment, just long enough for a joke.
—Herman Hesse, *Steppenwolf*

Since my house burned down,
I now have a better view
Of the rising moon.
—Masahide

Comedy is a more pervasive human condition than tragedy. Often we are or could be Quixotes or Tartuffes. Seldom are we Macbeths or Othellos.
—Wylie Sypher, *Our New Sense of the Comic*

The secret source of humor itself is not joy, but sorrow. There is no humor in heaven.
—Mark Twain

Laughs are exactly as honorable as tears. Laughter and tears are both responses to frustration and exhaustion, to the futility of thinking and striving anymore.
—Kurt Vonnegut, *Palm Sunday*

Jesus' terse comment that "whoever exalts himself will be humbled, and whoever humbles himself will be exalted." is not only a fundamental biblical theme but a fundamental theme in the history of comedy.
—Conrad Hyers, *And God Created Laughter*

Sympathizing Here

THE ROYAL WE

Friendship and Community

What's the most important thing in life? The Beatles summed it up like this: "All you need is love." Most movies and TV shows seem to agree. A life without love is a life not worth living.

The only problem, as any online dating service will reveal, is that love isn't all that easy to come by. Perhaps we should lower our expectations a bit and say "all you need is friends." Friendship makes a suitable alternative to love, and is much easier and less expensive to obtain. Remember: The Beatles also sang, "I get high with a little help from my friends." Friends are all you need.

However, because friendship produces far more subtle joys it's presumed somehow inferior to or less meaningful than love. Yet that's only true if you measure happiness in hormones; over the course of one's life, the overall value derived from a good friend can be far greater than that derived from a lover, spouse or offspring— especially in a modern era hallmarked by venereal disease, messy divorces, adolescent rebellion, and abundant Internet porn. Think of all the grief (and alimony) Paul McCartney could have avoided if he'd have merely Come Alone instead of Together.

True to its film noir roots, *The Big Lebowski* doesn't place much truck in romance—all the love-struck relationships in the film are stricken. Not only is the Big Lebowski's trophy wife cheating on him for cash, but his daughter loathes him and his widow emasculated him; Walter's pining for his ex-wife Cynthia is so dire he must compensate for it with aggression and artillery; the climactic "lovemaking" scene between Maude and the Dude turns out to be only a mercenary solicitation for sperm; and even the nihilists are fucked, man—Uli impels his girlfriend to cut off her toe so they can extract a phony ransom. It's not fair!

Yet, where *The Big Lebowski* differs from film noir is that it offers an alternative to love—namely friendship and community. Iconic private investigators like Phillip Marlowe and Sam Spade were tragic figures because they were cast utterly alone against a bleak dystopian landscape; the Dude on the other hand is spared the black hole of nihilism by his association in a bowling league and trying-but-true pals like

Walter, Donny, and Marty the landlord. It makes him (and us by extension) feel all warm inside.

Thus, what is the answer to the existential dread written about by dour modern philosophers like Sartre and Nietzsche? Navigating the Seven Cs—Companions, compeers, compassion, calmness, comedy, cocktails (or cannabis) and sporting competition. Love may make the world go round, as the saccharine saying goes, but friendship makes the ride a whole lot less bumpy. It's like Lennon said: "I am he as you are he as you are me and we are all together." J.W. Lennon! *Goo goo g'dude.*

Donny nearly had it: *We* are the walrus.

He who would do great things should not attempt them all alone.
—*American Indian Proverb*

And I say to you that we are full of chemicals which require us to belong to folk societies, or failing that, to feel lousy all the time. We are chemically engineered to live in folk societies, just as fish are chemically engineered to live in clean water...

When anything happens to us which would not happen in a folk society, our chemicals make us feel like fish out of water. Our chemicals demand that we get back into the water again. If we become increasingly wild and preposterous in modern times—well, so do fish on river banks, for a little while.

If we become increasingly apathetic in modern times—well, so do fish on river banks, after a little while. Our children often come to resemble apathetic fish—except that fish can't play guitars.
—Kurt Vonnegut, *Wampeters, Foma and Granfalloons*

The brain evolved to its large size because its information-processing capacity enabled humans to band together and increase their chances of survival. The size of a primate's brain correlates directly with the size of its social group, and the formula worked out by scientists indicates that the human brain is sized for a group of about 150, which by no coincidence is the number in a typical band of hunter-gatherers.
—John Tierney, *"Technology Makes Us Better," New York Times Magazine*, September 28, 1997

A friend is one who knows you and loves you just the same.
—Elbert Hubbard

In life, one is always alone. The important thing is to know with whom!
—Frédéric Dard

Anybody who is popular is bound to be disliked.
—Yogi Berra

He who is an idler without unsocial dispositions, finds occasional companions in all characters and professions.
—Henry Mackenzie.

A man cannot be a whole society to a woman, and a woman cannot be a whole society to a man. We try, but it is scarcely surprising that so many of us go to pieces.

So I recommend that everybody here join all sorts of organizations, no matter how ridiculous, simply to get more people in his or her life. It does not matter much if all the other members are morons. Quantities of relatives of any sort are what we need.
—Kurt Vonnegut, *Palm Sunday*

It is absurd to divide people into good and bad. People are either charming or tedious.
—Oscar Wilde

We do not need the help of our friends so much as the confidence that our friends will help us.
—Epicurus

There are no special orders of creatures called enemies or friends. Persons become friends or enemies according to the trend of circumstance.
—*The Mahabharata*

A rug is not woven from a single thread.
—Chinese Proverb

Our huge brains arose primarily to cope with the enormous complexity of dealing with each other; the primary adaptation of our species is not hunting, toolmaking or language, but our ability to cooperate. Ultimately, my research revealed that our species' remarkable evolutionary success is due to a trait that most of us take for granted, but that is rare among other animals on this planet: We make friends.
—William Allman, *The Stone Age Present*

I destroy my enemies when I make them my friends.
—Abraham Lincoln

It is one of the blessings of old friends that you can afford to be stupid with them.
—Ralph Waldo Emerson

I'd rather have friends who care than friends who agree with me.
—Arlo Guthrie

Erik Erikson coined the term "pseudo-speciation" to describe our xenophobic instinct. It is as if we rejected out of hand the unity of the species, setting up in its place a thousand egregious dichotomies.
—Melvin Konner, *Why the Reckless Survive*

Abraham Lincoln: Fourscore and...
    [looks at his pocket watch]
Abraham Lincoln: ...seven minutes ago...we, your forefathers, were brought forth upon a most excellent adventure conceived by our new friends, Bill...and Ted. These two great gentlemen are dedicated to a proposition which was true in my time, just as it's true today. Be excellent to each other. And...PARTY ON, DUDES!
—From *Bill and Ted's Excellent Adventure (1989)*. Screenplay by Chris Matheson and Ed Solomon

The best way to cheer yourself up is to try to cheer somebody else up.
—Mark Twain

Much of our communal life seems to be a lying contest.
—David Mamet, *Three Uses of the Knife*

Friendship requires more time than poor busy men can usually command.
—Ralph Waldo Emerson

Men come together to live; they remain together to live the good life.
—Aristotle

Who has but once dined with his friends, has tasted what it is to be a Caesar.
—Herman Melville, *Moby Dick*

We should look for someone to eat and drink with before looking for something to eat and drink, for dining alone is leading the life of a lion or wolf.
—Epicurus

My outline...is also the inline of the world.
—Alan Watts, *Psychotherapy, East and West*

"What's the use of dying in a ward surrounded by a lot of groaning and croaking incurables? Wouldn't it be much better to throw a party with that twenty-seven thousand and take poison and depart for the other world to the sound of violins, surrounded by lovely drunken girls and happy friends?"
—Mikhail Bulgakov, *The Master and Margarita*

A friend may well be reckoned the masterpiece of nature.
—Ralph Waldo Emerson

Stupefyin'

IT REALLY TIED THE ROOM TOGETHER

The Dudeiverse

Astronomy and physics have been pretty hard on the human ego. It wasn't long ago that the best scientists in the land believed that humans lived in the dead center of everything that was. Then Copernicus and Galileo came along and the universe, as we understood it, began to expand rapidly. Suddenly the sun was at the center, then the galaxy, then the concept of "center" became immaterial. Now we know that the universe so big that our feeble brains cannot begin to comprehend it (the occasional acid flashback notwithstanding). Moreover, there may even be many more universes— an infinite number even, increasing a trillionfold every nanosecond. It's enough to drive one to nihilism. Say what you will.

As we've noted, there are many theories about comedy. One of the most popular says that something is funny when our expectations don't match up with real-world results. Put in Dudeist terms: the rug that tied the room together has been pulled out from under us and we laugh to release our anguish. As Walter Sobchak eloquently put it: "Well it's, sometimes the cathartic, uh." Comedy shrinks the horror of humiliation into something small enough to bear.

This in mind, what shall we do to deal with this galactic humiliation laid before us? Namely, the fact that we now know that our species is an infinitesimally tiny thread in merely one of an infinite number of inconceivably enormous cosmic rugs?

There's only one thing to do, of course—laugh about it. In fact, the common assertion that our meaninglessness in the grand scheme of things might be cause for disappointment surely makes no sense. Our meaninglessness in the face of the infinite makes our condition so much easier to take. Life is a ruse. A farce! A shaggy dog story! There never was any fucking money. She kidnapped herself. *Fuggeddaboutit*. Losing a million dollars from the back seat of your rusted Ford Torino seems a lot less vexing when projected upon the big screen of eternity.

And yet, there's another side to all this. While our humanity may only be accidental, we also learn from our accidents. That is to say, we evolve by reinvesting. As the principle of compound interest suggests, reinvesting can lead to huge things over time. There's a fun illustration others have pointed out: Everyone says the Indians got a raw deal for Manhattan, but the 20 dollars that the Dutch paid them in 1626 would be worth more than Manhattan today if it had been invested in a 5% interest-bearing account.

By reinvesting their discoveries via love and language into our culture over the eons, smarter fellers than ourselves have soldiered on and eventually taken these hills, reaching a vantage point over all the tumbling tumbleweeds in the valleys below. In using our humility to say "fuck it" to falling down, avoid uptight thinking, and help keep our mind limber, humanity has unraveled some of the craziest cases of all time.

And yet it never gets wrapped up. The more we learn, the more we find out we don't know. It's a neverending story and there is no final answer. Which is why our cosmic insignificance is in fact a gift, for it frees us from the impossible job of having to figure out our place in the universe. Now that we know that we don't have a particular objective or meaning or purpose or "place" and furthermore that there may be an infinite number of universes in which we are irrelevant in, we can more fully appreciate our private residence (Earth) and perhaps try to tie our room together a bit better.

This is not to say that we should believe in nothing. The opposite, in fact: we should stop wasting time believing in things which are not. After which we can allow ourselves to spend more time at play. This is what, after all, according to modern physics and eastern philosophy, the universe has always done. What are atomic particles but tiny bowling balls rolling and crashing over and over to produce a cascade of gutters and strikes, league games and tournaments, in one great big round-robin that never ends? It's fucking interesting, man. It's all just a game, man. And yet so much more interesting (and compound interesting) than the fascist alternatives which falsely and often disastrously claim to know all the answers.

The saddest thing about our anthropocentric "fall from grace," it seems, wasn't the ensuing loss of self-importance, but realizing how much time and energy our ancestors wasted fretting over absolutely nothing. They were at the controls of an imaginary machine, laboring intensely at a job for which they had never actually been hired. That sounds exhausting. Had they known how ludicrous their story was, they would have just said "fuck it" and gone bowling. Let's not make the same mistake! Life is too short and too amazing to be put in a box.

The Indonesians traditionally believe that the universe is formed by the warp and woof of god's thread busily weaving a cosmic design. Many traditional cultures use the carding, spinning, and weaving processes of fabric-making as an analogy for universal creation.
—Katya Walker, *The Tao of Chaos*

Nature uses only the longest threads to weave her patterns, so each small piece of her fabric reveals the organization of the entire tapestry.
—Richard Feynman

To summarize the significant features of the quantum revolution, we find that rigid laws of motion are really a myth. Matter is allowed to roam more or less at random, subject to certain pressures, such as the reluctance to engage in too much activity. Complete chaos is thus averted because matter is lazy as well as undisciplined, so that in a sense the universe avoids total disintegration because of the inherent indolence of nature.
—Paul Davies, *Other Worlds*

The ideal would be to make each thing the center of the universe. And this is what the depth of something means: what there is in it of reflection of other things, allusion to other things.
—José Ortega y Gasset, *Meditations on Quixote*

What is the ultimate truth about ourselves? Various answers suggest themselves. We are a bit of stellar matter gone wrong. We are physical machinery—puppets that strut and talk and laugh and die as the hand of time pulls the strings beneath. But there is one elementary inescapable answer. *We are that which asks the question.*
—Arthur Eddington

You know, bowling takes on this almost religious significance because it's so much like a religion. I mean the ball is round, like the earth, and it's got the holy trinity: the Father, the Son, and the...Thumbhole. And as you roll the ball down the alley of life...Striking out the pagan religions of the past...Sparing them the anguish of their lives in the gutter...Framing their existence in an eternal metaphysicalness. Something like a 7-10 split!
—The Arrogant Worms, *"Let's Go Bowling"*

Not tame and gentle bliss, but disaster, heroically encountered, is man's true happy ending.
—Lewis Mumford, *Herman Melville*

There ain't no answer. There ain't going to be any answer. There never has been an answer. That's the answer.
—Gertrude Stein

Nobody needs to pay for the universe. It is the ultimate free lunch.
—Paul Davies

All humans will die. As they were at the birth of the Universe, all elements will be free of sin again.
—Kurt Vonnegut, *Timequake*

It would seem that the universe is 30 billion light years across and every inch of it would kill us if we went there. This is the position of the universe with regard to human life.
—Martin Amis, *The Information*

There are certain queer times and occasions in this strange mixed affair we call life when a man takes this whole universe for a vast practical joke, though the wit thereof he but dimly discerns, and more than suspects that the joke is at nobody's expense but his own.
—Herman Melville, *Moby Dick*

The story so far: In the beginning, the Universe was created. This has made a lot of people very angry and has been widely regarded as a bad move.
—Douglas Adams, *The Restaurant at the End of the Universe*

There is a crack in everything. That's how the light gets in.
—Leonard Cohen

The Universe is change; life is opinion.
—Marcus Aurelius

God made everything out of nothing, but the nothingness shows through.
—Paul Valéry

Once you can accept the universe as matter expanding into nothing that is something, wearing stripes with plaid comes easy.
—Albert Einstein

In the end, everything is a gag.
—Charlie Chaplin

...the primary reason it is so difficult to achieve happiness centers on the fact that, contrary to the myths mankind has developed to reassure itself, the universe was not created to answer our needs. Frustration is deeply woven into the fabric of life. And whenever some of our needs *are* temporarily met, we immediately start wishing for more. This chronic dissatisfaction is the second obstacle that stands in the way of contentment.
—Mihaly Csikszentmihalyi, *Flow: The Psychology of Optimal Experience*

Every so often, I like to stick my head out the window, look up, and smile for a satellite picture.
—Stephen Wright

Those who would have good government without its correlative misrule, and without its correlative wrong, do not understand the principles of the universe.
—Alan Watts, *Beat Zen, Square Zen, and Zen*

Even sleepers are workers and collaborators on what goes on in the universe.
—Heraclitus

The archbattle in the universe is always: evolution versus egocentricism. The evolutionary drive to produce greater depth is synonymous with the drive to overcome egocentricism, to find wider and deeper wholes, to unfold greater and greater unions. A molecule overcomes the egocentricism of an atom. A cell overcomes the egocentricism of a molecule. And nowhere is this trend more obvious than in human development itself.
—Ken Wilber, *A Brief History of Everything*

I have an existential map. It has "You are here" written all over it.
—Steven Wright

The Dudescent of Man

FURTHER ON DOWN THE TRAIL

Dudevolution

Though commonly pictured with a grim scowl and a heavy brow (perhaps it bore the burden of mankind's broken dreams), Charles Darwin was in fact quite the Dude.

In fact, aside from coming up with the theory of evolution, Darwin's life is proof of another natural process at work in some of our lives: *Dudevolution*.

Like many dudes, in his early life Darwin was a misfit in school. First he failed in his studies to become a doctor. Then he failed in his studies to become an Anglican priest. His aristocratic parents worried that he was a loser, a deadbeat, a bum. And he was! Yet that's only because he had not yet found his niche.

One of the important lessons of Darwin's Theory of Natural Selection is that among organisms there is no such thing as "better" or "worse"—only "well-adapted" or "poorly adapted" to one's environment. The same goes for Dudevolution.

Some folks adapt swimmingly to the mind-molding imposed upon us during thirteen years of mandatory schooling. Others adapt poorly—usually for one of two reasons: either a) they don't care about learning at all, or b) Like the young French poet Rimbaud, they recognize at an early age that "True life is elsewhere."

It is this latter group that we're concerned with here, because these are the folks who often go on to become Great Dudes in History. Their reluctance or inability to adapt obliges them to drive their "wagons westward" in search of a train of thought that really hitches their lives together. (Note, of course, that one does not have to do poorly in school to become a Dude—Dudes are often found high up at the head of the class, though they are often criticized for having their heads in the clouds.)

This is the situation young Darwin found himself in. After failing so miserably in the fields that his loving parents chose for him, Charlie finally went eyeball-to-eyeball with what he was actually interested in. And that was bugs.

Darwin's interest in collecting insects became so ardent that it drew the attention of a professor of Natural Science at his university who suggested he join a voyage around the world aboard the HMS Beagle to collect specimens. The rest is history. Darwin spent five years observing species of animals all over the planet. After discovering how they had adapted perfectly to their environmental niches, he came up with his Theory of Natural Selection, or "evolution," in the parlance of our times. Once he was in his element, he himself evolved from a dope to a pope. Son of a niche!

As we mentioned before, it's a common mistake to assume that Dudeism is all about being lazy. Rather, Dudeism is all about maintaining personal freedom in the face of tremendous pressure to conform to society's expectations. Yet since one of society's most strident expectations is that you work hard to achieve a preordained set of challenges, the rebel shrug of "takin 'er easy" will always remain an important element in the Dudeist evolutionary strategy.

Of course, like Darwin, Dudeists are not all deadbeats. A look at the Great Dudes in History sections at The Church of the Latter-Day Dude and its magazine *The Dudespaper*[10] makes clear that it's not a person's indolence that makes a dude, but their independence of thought. That, and a pair of ventricles: A true dude must have a good heart too. Independence without compassion leads to sociopathies such as violence, nihilism and crappy modern art.

Dudes by definition are always on the fringes of social ecosystem, which can sometimes make them seem like losers or bums, people the square community doesn't give a shit about. However, it's just the opposite: their fringe thinking is what leads to most of the cultural evolution we enjoy. Just as with biological evolution, all it takes is one organism to develop a cool new adaptation before it rapidly spreads throughout the species. This is why it's good to know they're out there takin' it easy for us sinners—Dudes like Darwin limberly crack cases to mysteries the rest of us lack the perspective or freedom to even dream of.

---

[10] www.dudeism.com/greatdudes and www.dudespaper.com

The reasonable man adapts himself to the world: the unreasonable one persists in trying to adapt the world to himself. Therefore all progress depends on the unreasonable man.
—George Bernard Shaw, *Maxims for Revolutionists*

It seems the more evolved an animal is, the more time it spends playing. Which does not explain why I'm at the typewriter, unless it does.
—P. J. O'Rourke, *All the Trouble in the World*

It is nonsense to try to think of any individual organism in isolation as "alive." Isolate a human being, or any other living thing, from its environment, and within a very short time that organism would be dead. The only genuinely *living* system that we know of from our own direct experience is the entire biosphere of the Earth.
—John Gribbin, *In the Beginning*

Everybody makes mistakes, but it's how you handle them that makes you a role model.
—Reba McEntire

While the process of evolution is often characterized in terms of dog-eat-dog competition and the "survival of the fittest," this new research also reveals that, in fact, nice guys often finish first. Our species' success over the eons is due to the fact that we are the most *cooperative* creatures on earth.
—William Allman, *The Stone Age Present*

There is no salvation in becoming adapted to a world which is crazy.
—Henry Miller

Many [earthlings] were increasingly of the opinion that they'd all made a big mistake in coming down from the trees in the first place. And some said that even the trees had been a bad move, and that no one should ever have left the oceans.
—Douglas Adams, *The Hitchhiker's Guide to the Galaxy*

People cannot be adapted to the present, or the future; they can only be adapted to the past.
—Matt Ridley, *The Red Queen*

In order for the wheel to turn, for life to be lived, impurities are needed, and the impurities of impurities in the soil, too, as is known, if it is to be fertile. Dissention, diversity, the grain of salt and mustard are needed. Fascism does not want them, forbids them…it wants everyone to be the same, and you're not.
—Primo Levi, *The Periodic Table*

Except during the nine months before he draws his first breath, no man manages his affairs as well as a tree does.
—George Bernard Shaw

Weaseling out of things is important to learn. It's what separates us from the animals…except the weasel.
—Homer Simpson, *The Simpsons*, Season 5, Episode 8. Script by Dan McGrath

The vaunted progress of life is really random motion away from simple beginnings, not directed impetus towards inherently advantageous complexity.
—Stephen Jay Gould, *Full House*

Imagination is more important than knowledge. For knowledge is limited, whereas imagination embraces the entire world, stimulating progress, giving birth to evolution.
—Albert Einstein

Maybe the target nowadays is not to discover what we are, but to refuse what we are.
—Michel Foucault

Life is like playing a violin solo in public and learning the instrument as one goes on.
—Samuel Butler

In the long run we are all dead.
—John Maynard Keynes

Our ancestors may have started to walk tall to stay cool.
—Chris Stringer and Robin McKie, *African Exodus*

"I know at last what I want to be when I grow up. When I grow up I want to be a little boy."
—Joseph Heller, *Something Happened.*

The thing the sixties did was to show us the possibilities and the responsibility that we all had. It wasn't the answer. It just gave us a glimpse of the possibility.
—John Lennon

Or maybe the Beat Generation, which is the offspring of the Lost Generation, is just another step towards that last, pale generation which will not know the answers either.
—Jack Kerouac, *"About the Beat Generation"*

Such sports as baseball, football, wrestling, track and field events, chess and warfare may owe their appeal—as well as their largely male following—to these prewired hunting skills, which served us so well for millions of years of human history but which find diminished practical applications today.
—Carl Sagan, *The Dragons of Eden*

I myself are not a perfected system—never will be, since my own life is in continual evolution—so why should any other system be perfect?
—Katya Walker, *The Tao of Chaos*

Adults are just obsolete children and the hell with them.
—Theodor Geisel (Dr. Seuss)

Life is a near-death experience.
—George Carlin

SPECIAL BONUS CHAPTER:

THIS WAS A VALUED, UH, UH

The Kerouac Rug Mystery

Then [Jack Kerouac had] moved into [William] Burroughs house in Algiers where he'd stolen the only thing of value that Burroughs had in it, the rug. As [Burroughs] wrote Allen [Ginsberg] every time he looked at the bare floor he was "...put in mind of his vile act."
—Ann Charters and Allen Ginsberg, *Kerouac, A Biography*

Every American wants MORE MORE of the world and why not, you only live once. But the mistake made in America is persons accumulate more more dead matter, machinery, possessions and rugs and fact information at the expense of what really counts for more: feeling, good feeling, sex feeling, tenderness feeling, mutual feeling. You own twice as much rug if you're twice as aware of the rug.
—Allen Ginsberg, *Letter to The Wall Street Journal, 1966*

Wasn't it Jack Kerouac that said, "Even if I have a rug I have too much"?
—Jake Vig, *Confidence (2003)*. Screenplay by Doug Jung

Made in the USA
Lexington, KY
10 December 2015